STRATEGY IN EVERYDAY LIFE

THE UNAUTHORIZED MBA OF BEING HUMAN

NAVOCH MOHANAYAK

Clever Fox® PUBLISHING
Chennai • Bangalore

CLEVER FOX PUBLISHING
Chennai, India

Published by CLEVER FOX PUBLISHING 2026

ISBN: 978-93-7500-276-5

Dedication

To Nameeta,

who has lived this book more patiently than she ever needed to.

For every dishwasher standoff, every overanalyzed dinner conversation, and every time you endured a "framework" when all you wanted was silence — thank you for being both data and delight.

You are the only stakeholder whose approval truly mattered, the only long-term merger that never required a term sheet, and the quiet strategist behind every sentence that pretends to be clever.

To you — for the laughter that steadied the satire, the grace that made the chaos bearable, and the love that refused to be optimized.

(Also dedicated, in smaller print, to caffeine, confusion, and the Wi-Fi router — without whom this book would have been finished months earlier, but much less honestly.)

FOREWORD

In Praise of Overthinking, Elegantly

by **Someone Who Really Should Know Better**

It is a truth universally acknowledged that a person in possession of a functioning Wi-Fi connection must be in want of a framework.

That, I suspect, is how *Strategy in Everyday Life* happened — not as an act of creation, but as a coping mechanism.

For years, I've known Navoch Mohanayak to be that rare hybrid of strategist and satirist: a man capable of delivering a 12-slide deck on "household alignment" before realizing he's still wearing mismatched socks.

He is, in short, the only person I know who can apply Porter's Five Forces to the act of making tea — and still arrive late to the meeting about it.

The Curious Case of the Author

Mohanayak is the sort of man who sees the world not as it is, but as a badly managed organization trying to meet its quarterly KPIs. Where others see chaos, he sees a dashboard. Where others see relationships, he sees mergers. Where others see family, he sees a hostile boardroom with shared assets and differing appetites for risk.

His friends claim this is what makes him fascinating. His family claims this is what makes him exhausting. Both are correct.

In conversation, he oscillates between the confidence of a management consultant and the humility of someone who has lost control of his Google Calendar. He believes deeply in human irrationality, yet keeps scheduling logic into it. He's not a philosopher; he's a man trying to debug philosophy using Excel.

What You're About to Read

This book, I must warn you, is a trap.

It will begin innocently — a witty take on household chores or grocery shopping — and before you know it, you'll be knee-deep in a discussion about bounded rationality and emotional arbitrage.

You'll laugh first, then realize you're laughing at yourself. And then, like any good strategy document, you'll begin to doubt your life choices.

Strategy in Everyday Life is not a parody of management thinking; it's an affectionate dissection of it. Navoch doesn't mock strategy — he humanizes it. He turns frameworks into folklore, decisions into data points, and the act of living into a series of brilliant, stupid experiments.

The result is a strange and beautiful hybrid: part behavioral economics, part stand-up comedy, part philosophical diary written by a man who can't stop taking notes on his own misfortunes.

Why This Book Matters (Even If It Shouldn't)

The modern world, as Navoch correctly observes, has become a conference call with no agenda. We navigate complexity with buzzwords, apply design thinking to lunch plans, and pivot our happiness quarterly.

In such a world, humor isn't just an escape — it's a diagnostic tool. Navoch's essays invite us to examine our absurdity, not to fix it but to appreciate its design flaws.

He doesn't preach improvement. He practices acceptance — the kind that comes after three failed attempts and one well-worded apology email.

There's an emotional intelligence here that sneaks up on you. Beneath the wit, there's tenderness — a recognition that the frameworks we cling to are less about control and more about comfort. That "strategy" is, at its best, a story we tell ourselves to make the unpredictable feel navigable.

And that laughter, ultimately, is the only KPI that matters.

The Final Footnote

When I first read these essays, I caught myself doing something rare: *pausing.* Not to reflect on their cleverness (which is abundant), but to recognize the peculiar relief they offer — the permission to be analytical *and* absurd, insightful *and* inept, strategic *and* stupid.

In Navoch's universe, you can fail gloriously and still get a performance bonus for "creative resilience." You can overthink your way into self-awareness. You can lose every argument and still win a laugh.

So, dear reader, approach this book not as a manual, but as a mirror. You'll see yourself — ambitious, confused, overcaffeinated — and you'll finally understand that maybe, just maybe, this is what strategy was meant to be all along: a beautifully crafted excuse for doing our best despite knowing better.

Read it slowly. Laugh frequently. And when you find yourself nodding in recognition — remember, that's not agreement, that's empathy.

– [Name Redacted by Request]

(Strategist, reader, occasional writer.)

PREFACE

Why This Book Exists — and Why It Probably Shouldn't

The Problem with Strategy

The problem with "strategy" is that everyone thinks they need one — for their careers, their diets, their marriages, their mornings.

It used to be a corporate word, confined to boardrooms and PowerPoint decks filled with arrows, funnels, and hopeful verbs.

Then, one day, it escaped.

Now we are all strategists.

We strategize our relationships. We strategize our vacations. We strategize our "digital detoxes" with three productivity apps.

We don't just live anymore — we manage our existence like overworked CEOs of tiny, underperforming start-ups called *Our Lives Inc.*

Somewhere, between "vision statements" and "personal goals," the simple act of existing was quietly rebranded as *strategic alignment.*

This book is a rebellion against that. Or, perhaps, another symptom of it.

A Brief History of a Bad Idea

This project began — as all strategic initiatives do — with confusion and coffee.

One day, while arguing over who should load the dishwasher (a domestic standoff of epic, recurring proportions), it occurred to me that my family had unintentionally replicated a *non-cooperative equilibrium.*

It was pure game theory, played out in slippers and resentment.

The thought was amusing. Then unsettling. Then useful.

Because if game theory could explain household chores, perhaps every mundane frustration — from queueing at a supermarket to maintaining friendships — had a hidden strategy behind it.

And if strategy could explain life, surely life could return the favor.

That's how *Strategy in Everyday Life* began: as a joke, then an observation, then a joke again — a cycle that, frankly, describes most of human progress.

What This Book Is

This is as far a cry from being a self-help book as it can be.

The last thing it will do, and that too with reluctance, is optimize your mornings, monetize your mindfulness, or help you "win" at life (a phrase I deeply distrust). Instead, it's a mirror — albeit one that distorts, exaggerates, and occasionally winks.

Each essay begins in the everyday — a fight, a commute, a queue — and gradually inflates into a case study nobody asked for. It borrows from economics, psychology, and the darker corners of corporate jargon to reveal how absurdly strategic we've become — and how hopelessly human we remain.

The tone, I'll admit, is part satire, part confession. Because somewhere between my MBA notes and my personal chaos, I realized that the frameworks we use to "win" at business are the same ones that make us lose at life — just with better formatting.

What This Book Is Not

It is not an argument for cynicism. Nor is it a call to abandon structure and drift into chaos. Rather, it is a quiet invitation to see the comedy in our control.

Life, as it turns out, is not a zero-sum game — it's a badly run cooperative, where everyone keeps accidentally scheduling meetings for the same time slot.

This book doesn't solve that problem. It simply provides commentary from the back of the room.

How to Read This Book

You can read it linearly, like a syllabus for the world's most confused MBA.

Or you can dip into it, chapter by chapter, like a curious anthropologist studying the tribe of "modern adults under moderate stress."

There's no wrong way to read it — though, much like strategy implementation, there are plenty of inefficient ones.

Each chapter has been written to stand alone — a short essay, a quiet chuckle, a philosophical shrug. Together, they form a loose narrative about survival through self-awareness.

You might laugh. You might cringe. Occasionally, you might think, *"Oh no, that's me."* That's good. That's data.

The Underlying Hope

If this book has a secret agenda, it's to humanize strategy and dignify confusion.

To remind us that frameworks, models, and theories — however elegant — collapse the moment they meet a real human being with limited sleep and unlimited Wi-Fi.

Because at the heart of every business decision, every negotiation, every ambition, and every breakdown is the same messy operating system: emotion disguised as logic.

And that's not a flaw. It's the whole point.

Closing the Loop

So yes — this book probably shouldn't exist.

It's overthought, overstructured, and entirely too amused by itself. But then again, so is life.

If you're looking for answers, you won't find them here. But if you're looking for better questions, or better jokes about bad answers — welcome.

This is not the art of living well. It's the science of laughing at why we can't.

TABLE OF CONTENTS

NOTE TO THE READER

(Read before you attempt to apply any of this to your actual life)

This is not a guidebook. It's more like a travel diary written by someone who got lost on the way to productivity and decided to take notes instead.

The essays that follow were not designed to improve your efficiency, optimize your emotions, or make you a better person — though any of those outcomes would be a delightful accident. They were written in the spirit of mild exasperation, deep curiosity, and the unshakable suspicion that most of our daily struggles are just poorly marketed strategy problems.

You may find yourself nodding in agreement, laughing in recognition, or closing the book mid-chapter to rethink your life choices. That's normal. It's part of the methodology.

Please proceed with caution, compassion, and caffeine. And remember — if something here sounds profound, it's probably a joke. If it sounds like a joke, it's probably true.

Life as a Case Study in Strategic Confusion

If you've ever stared at a spreadsheet, a family calendar, or your own reflection and thought, "There must be a better way to manage this," you already qualify as a strategist — albeit an unpaid and emotionally unstable one.

Because that's what strategy really is: the persistent illusion that **clarity is achievable** if only we think hard enough.

For millennia, humans have been refining this illusion — from Sun Tzu's *Art of War* to modern management consultants charging $900 an hour to rename common sense as "synergistic foresight." But somewhere along the way, something strange happened: we started importing those same frameworks into our private lives.

Your colleague uses "Porter's Five Forces" to justify switching gyms. Your spouse applies "SWOT analysis" to dinner options. Your friend talks about "emotional ROI." Your parents manage family WhatsApp groups like multinational corporations.

We are living in the golden age of strategic delusion — and it's oddly comforting.

The Bi-Directional Flow of Nonsense

When I first began thinking about this project, I assumed it would be a satire — a send-up of the way corporate jargon seeps into everything. ("Our relationship needs better alignment on deliverables.")

But as I started mapping these patterns, I noticed something more interesting: the exchange goes both ways.

We borrow from business to understand life — *and* from life to make business bearable. Every framework in your office PowerPoint exists because someone, somewhere, once had to make sense of dinner with relatives.

Game theory? Born out of arguments between people who wanted to be right without being single. **Porter's Five Forces?** A poetic description of kitchen politics. **SWOT analysis?** The emotional process of deciding whether to confront your in-laws.

Conversely, everyday life offers its own quietly elegant management systems:

- **The queue at the supermarket** — a masterclass in behavioral operations.
- **The family WhatsApp group** — a live simulation of communication breakdown.
- **The sibling rivalry** — pure market segmentation with a dash of narcissism.

We don't *apply* frameworks to life; we *invented* them from life, then re-imported them in shinier fonts.

This book is, therefore, not satire — it's a field report from that borderland where seriousness collapses into comedy and emerges as wisdom.

On Everyday Strategy and the Myth of Rationality

Economists love the phrase *"rational actor."* It describes a mythical creature that always makes optimal decisions. In the wild, however, you'll find only *rationalizers* — humans who make terrible decisions and then construct PowerPoint slides to justify them.

We are *post hoc* strategists. We fall in love, buy things we don't need, stay in jobs that exhaust us, and then reverse-engineer these disasters into "growth experiences."

And that's the essence of everyday strategy: it's not planning — it's storytelling. We explain our chaos to ourselves using borrowed vocabulary until it sounds like a choice.

When we call it "resilience," what we often mean is "I've run out of options." When we call it "learning agility," we mean "I survived by accident." When we say "value creation," we're describing coffee.

We have, in other words, built an entire civilization on creative post-rationalization — and we're doing fine.

A Working Definition of Strategy (That Will Self-Destruct in Three Paragraphs)

Traditionalists define strategy as "the alignment of resources toward long-term objectives under conditions of uncertainty."

Which is elegant, but entirely unhelpful when your uncertainty involves a toddler, an Uber surge, and an existential crisis.

So here's mine:

Strategy is the art of pretending you had a plan.

It's the ability to give chaos a narrative arc — to rename improvisation as foresight. It's why we admire leaders, parents, and people who make confident eye contact while Googling "what to do next."

Every great strategist, at home or at work, is a world-class rebrander of panic.

The Everyday Case Study Method

If business schools have case studies on IBM, Apple, and Toyota, this book studies the true innovators:

- The parent negotiating with a five-year-old about bedtime (change management).
- The commuter deciding which lane will move faster (real options theory).
- The partner who uses silence as a communication strategy (nonverbal brinkmanship).
- The shopper comparing prices, coupons, and life choices in aisle six (behavioral economics).

Every chapter in this book is a management case study you've already lived — and probably failed.

You'll find no actionable insights here, only comforting patterns of failure and the reassurance that everyone's pretending equally hard.

Why Humor Works Better Than Vision Statements

Humor, as I've come to understand it, is the only management tool that scales infinitely. It costs nothing, offends almost everyone equally, and produces measurable reductions in existential despair.

Where PowerPoints demand attention, humor invites reflection. Where strategy aims for precision, humor thrives in ambiguity. Where corporate life says, *"Control the variables,"* humor whispers, *"Good luck with that."*

So I write not to instruct, but to *interrupt* — the rhythm of certainty that passes for wisdom in our daily lives.

If you laugh while reading, excellent — that means you recognized yourself. If you groan, even better — that means you're still trying.

The Point, If There Must Be One

This book is not about finding meaning in the mundane. It's about realizing that the mundane *is* the meaning — and we've been managing it badly.

Strategy isn't a corporate artifact; it's a survival instinct with a PowerPoint addiction. It's how we turn accidents into achievements and Monday mornings into motivational slides.

By studying it in its natural habitat — the kitchen, the traffic jam, the queue, the WhatsApp group — we might recover some humility about what we actually control: not much, and not for long.

And yet, we strategize anyway. Because to be human is to overestimate our agency and then write a charming essay about it.

The Invitation

So here's my invitation: Put away your MBA mindset. Forget frameworks as commandments. Think of them instead as metaphors — or coping mechanisms that went corporate.

Read each essay not as advice, but as a mirror — one that distorts just enough to make you laugh before you recognize yourself.

And if, by the end, you find yourself quoting this book earnestly in a meeting, don't worry. That, too, is part of the experiment.

After all, *life is the only boardroom where everyone eventually gets fired — and somehow, the coffee still runs out first.*

ARC I: THE HOME AS THE FIRST BOARDROOM

STRATEGY BEGINS WHERE WI-FI IS WEAK

CHAPTER I

THE DISHWASHER DILEMMA: GAME THEORY FOR THE DOMESTIC SOUL

> *Or: Why every relationship eventually becomes a case study in operational alignment.*

I. The Situation

It always starts innocently. Dinner's over. Plates stacked. Silence descends — the calm before the passive-aggressive storm.

You open the dishwasher door, confident, purposeful — a commander inspecting the battlefield. You load plates by category, angle the spoons scientifically, place the bowls in perfect geometric harmony. You step back, admire your work.

Then your partner enters. They smile vaguely, say something disarmingly casual like, "Oh, I'll just move this one to make more space," — and before you know it, the entire logistical equilibrium of your universe has collapsed.

The forks are now diagonal. The cups are upside down. The delicate system you perfected through years of unacknowledged genius lies in ruins.

You're not angry, you tell yourself — you're *disappointed.* Which, as every strategist knows, is the more scalable emotion.

II. The Model: The Domestic Prisoner's Dilemma

At its core, the dishwasher isn't about dishes. It's about **trust, ego, and control disguised as hygiene.**

In classical Game Theory, the *Prisoner's Dilemma* describes how two rational agents acting in self-interest can produce collectively irrational results.

In the *Domestic Variant*, it's the same — except neither agent is rational, and both believe they are.

Here's the model:

Decision	You cooperate	You defect
Partner cooperates	Peace and mild smugness	Minor annoyance; silent reloading at midnight
Partner defects	Loud sighs, performative martyrdom	Mutual escalation; long-term emotional attrition

Every couple eventually discovers the **Pareto-optimal point of fatigue** — where both silently agree to tolerate inefficiency in exchange for peace. This is known as *Equilibrium by Resignation.*

Or, in behavioral economics: *the optimal outcome when one party runs out of will to care.*

III. Anecdotal Case Study: The Plate Alignment Crisis

During lockdown, a couple — let's call them *Raj* and *Nisha* — found themselves in the throes of what anthropologists now call "Dishwasher Cold War I."

Raj believed in *vertical alignment for superior water circulation.* Nisha believed in *creative stacking for maximum capacity.*

They tried compromise. It lasted three days. By Day Four, they had developed parallel systems: Raj would "inspect" post-loading, Nisha would "forget" to close the door fully so he'd see the arrangement.

On Day Seven, Raj presented a spreadsheet labeled *Dishwasher Load Efficiency Analysis (v2.1)*. Nisha presented divorce papers in Comic Sans.

They are now happily married again — to each other – and their home has two hand-wash sinks.

IV. The Behavioral Breakdown

Why does a small domestic task provoke such grand emotion?

Because the dishwasher is a **stage for invisible hierarchies** — competence, validation, gratitude. Every plate becomes a proxy war for something else: acknowledgment, fairness, or simply the desperate need to prove we're doing life right.

Psychologists call this **the moralization of method** — when procedural correctness becomes moral superiority. We confuse *being right* with *being righteous.*

Hence the sighs, the sarcastic thank-yous, the solemn vow to "just do it myself next time." Every household has its own minor religion. The dishwasher is merely the altar.

V. Archetypes of the Domestic Strategist

Archetype	Core Belief	Tactical Behavior
The Process Purist	There is one correct way (mine)	Relabels utensils as "assets"
The Benevolent Overlord	"Let me fix that for you"	Equates help with hegemony

Archetype	Core Belief	Tactical Behavior
The Chaotic Optimist	"It'll wash somehow"	Lives by vibes, dies by mold
The Passive Resister	"I don't know how this works"	Weaponized incompetence
The Zen Dropout	"The dishes will find their path"	Outsources both effort and guilt

Margin note: "Every home has a Six Sigma practitioner and a saboteur. Sometimes they're married."

VI. The Strategic Takeaway: Pareto Peace Theory

Every household eventually stabilizes along what I call the **Domestic Pareto Curve** — where incremental improvements in cleanliness no longer justify the emotional cost of insisting on them.

Mathematically:

Peace = Function (Tolerance ÷ Optimization)

As tolerance increases, optimization decreases — and happiness goes up. At equilibrium, one partner sighs theatrically, the other pretends not to notice, and both secretly reload later when no one's watching.

This is not hypocrisy; it's **adaptive diplomacy**. The corporate equivalent would be "delegation with silent audit."

VII. The Corporate Parallel

Every organization has its own dishwasher problem. Leaders preach empowerment, but quietly "fix" their teams' slides before presentations. Managers insist on ownership — but rewrite every bullet in the deck.

They call it *quality control.* It's actually *ego laundering.*

The result is familiar:

- The doer feels infantilized.
- The fixer feels unappreciated.
- The outcome is functional mediocrity packaged as collaboration.

Corporates, like couples, survive not by perfect alignment — but by perfecting **the art of controlled imperfection.**

VIII. Anecdote Two: The Agile Kitchen Initiative

A Bangalore household once attempted to implement *Agile Scrum Methodology* for chores. They created a Kanban board on the fridge labeled: *To Wash*, *In Progress*, *Drying*, *Put Away*.

Week 1 went smoothly. Week 2 saw scope creep. By Week 3, "Done" was redefined as "Out of sight." The sprint review ended in mutiny when someone added a sticky note reading:

"This meeting could've been a nap."

Scrum was suspended indefinitely. The dishwasher continued on waterfall model.

IX. The Existential Undercurrent

The dishwasher is never really about dishes. It's about the ache for order in a world that resists it. The illusion that if we can just align the spoons perfectly, maybe everything else will click into place too — our routines, our work, our relationships, our purpose.

It's not insanity; it's strategy. We impose systems on chaos because it's easier than confronting our own mess.

Perhaps that's what love really is — the recurring willingness to reload each other's mistakes, quietly, and still call it teamwork.

X. The Moral (Still Dripping)

Every home has two types of people: those who optimize, and those who tolerate the optimizers. The real harmony lies not in the method, but in the mercy.

Moral: In both households and boardrooms, the greatest efficiency gain comes from learning to let it go.

"Domestic Systems Efficiency Index (DSEI) 2025"

According to the Institute of Applied Household Economics, 78% of couples report "minor procedural disputes" over dishwashing, 42% confess to "secret reloading," and 11% have considered parallel dishwashers. Longitudinal data shows a strong correlation between dishwasher diplomacy and overall relational longevity.

CHAPTER II

KITCHEN POLITICS AND POWER DYNAMICS: PORTER'S FIVE FORCES OF DINNER

> *Or: How every household meal is a case study in supply chain management and emotional leverage.*

I. The Situation

It's 7:45 p.m. Dinner time.

The air carries faint notes of cumin, coriander, and tension. Somewhere, a parent is yelling "Two minutes!" while everyone else is calculating escape velocity from their current tasks.

At the center of it all stands the cook — the **Household CEO** — stirring, tasting, multitasking, and silently rehearsing tonight's *Performance Review of Family Gratitude.*

Across the table, the consumers — known in organizational literature as *dependents* — prepare for evaluation. They're nervous. Not because of the food, but because they must now deliver their **quarterly feedback**: sincere enough to avoid insult, but vague enough to prevent requests for elaboration.

Dinner begins. A spoon clinks. Someone says, "It's… nice."

The CEO squints. There will be a post-mortem.

II. The Model: Porter's Five Forces of Dinner

Michael Porter, the management philosopher who once dissected industries into "competitive forces," never met an Indian kitchen — but he would've felt right at home.

Because the family dinner table is, in fact, the **perfect microeconomy**: a high-stakes market of labor, demand, negotiation, and deeply personal sabotage.

Let's adapt the model:

Porter's Force	Domestic Equivalent	Strategic Implication
1. Threat of New Entrants	Anyone else trying to "help cook."	Creates chaos, dilutes expertise, increases shouting.
2. Bargaining Power of Suppliers	Grocery budget & availability.	Determines menu mood: "Paneer night" vs "Dal of Resentment."
3. Bargaining Power of Buyers	Family members' appetites and unsolicited opinions.	Drives emotional volatility and culinary revenge.
4. Threat of Substitutes	Ordering in.	Undermines morale; triggers legacy insecurity.
5. Competitive Rivalry	Comparisons to "how mom used to make it."	Results in existential collapse of authority.

Each night's dinner is an open market. Everyone claims to want variety, but secretly craves predictability — the corporate equivalent of demanding innovation without changing a single process.

III. Anecdotal Case Study: The Paneer Mutiny

Consider *The Rajas.* A middle-class family in Delhi, united by love and divided by palate.

Mrs. Raja, culinary monarch and chief procurement officer, decided to innovate — switching from regular paneer curry to "paneer quinoa fusion." Her teenage son revolted immediately. Her husband tried diplomacy ("Interesting texture"). Her daughter quietly texted for pizza.

By the time dinner ended, there were three meals, two arguments, and one lonely bowl of quinoa.

The lesson was clear: in family markets, **innovation must be pre-approved by the target demographic.** Otherwise, it's not strategy. It's hubris.

IV. The Behavioral Breakdown

Dinner, at its core, is not about food. It's about *power disguised as nourishment.*

Feeding people is both the most intimate and the most political act — an everyday referendum on care, control, and competence.

Psychologists call this **nurturant dominance** — when love expresses itself through micromanagement. You can see it everywhere:

- "Have one more roti" = *Compliance testing.*
- "You didn't like it?" = *Feedback threat disguised as curiosity.*
- "Next time I won't make it at all" = *Emotional blackmail with garnish.*

Dinner, then, is strategy by other means — with coriander as collateral.

V. Archetypes of Kitchen Power

Archetype	Core Belief	Typical Behavior
The Culinary Autocrat	"My kitchen, my rules."	Delegates nothing, blames everyone.
The Democratic Disaster	"Let's all decide together!"	Creates chaos, eats last.
The Martyr Chef	"I do everything for you ungrateful people."	Peak performance under duress.
The Silent Rebel	"I'll just order food."	Weaponizes apathy.
The Outsourced Optimist	"Swiggy understands me better."	Believes freedom is one app away.

🗨 *Margin note:* "Behind every loving meal lies an unspoken SWOT analysis."

VI. The Strategic Takeaway: Kitchen as Power Economy

If *The Dishwasher Dilemma* was about cooperation, *Kitchen Politics* is about control. The key insight: **In domestic systems, authority doesn't flow from role — it flows from resource ownership.**

Who controls the groceries, controls the mood. Who sets the menu, controls the narrative. Who decides what's "healthy," controls the ideology.

This is **Porter's Hidden Sixth Force: Emotional Leverage.** The ability to convert affection into compliance through sustained calorie management.

Smart households evolve into **cooperative oligopolies** — each stakeholder owning a niche (budgeting, chopping, serving, pretending to like it). The inefficient ones? They collapse into **culinary dictatorships** — efficient, terrifying, and briefly delicious.

VII. The Corporate Parallel

Organizations aren't much different. Projects, like meals, are overcooked by too many stakeholders and under-seasoned by clear decision-making.

- The CEO wants creativity, but within the menu of precedent.
- The manager demands feedback, then takes offense when it's given.
- The intern (read: youngest child) keeps suggesting pizza.

Meetings become buffets where everyone eats but no one digests.

Just as the kitchen punishes dissent with hunger, the corporate world punishes honesty with silence. And both reward obedience with dessert.

VIII. Anecdote Two: The Agile Dinner Framework

A tech couple once tried to "modernize" mealtime. They implemented the **Agile Dinner Sprint Model**:

- Morning stand-ups ("What do we feel like eating tonight?")
- Rapid prototyping (half-cooked ideas in literal form)
- Feedback loops ("Could use more salt and emotional support")

After two weeks, they reverted to Waterfall Methodology: One person decides everything. Everyone else complains.

Agile failed because, as in real life, **iteration is easy — accountability isn't.**

IX. The Existential Undercurrent

The kitchen is civilization's oldest boardroom. It's where strategy began — fire management, resource allocation, alliance-building, survival.

Every dinner carries the echo of that primal negotiation: Who eats first, who eats best, who cleans afterward.

Perhaps that's why food carries such moral weight. It's not just consumption; it's belonging — the reassurance that someone, somewhere, still wants you nourished, even if it kills them.

X. The Moral (Simmered Down)

You can outsource cuisine, but not compassion. And no matter how efficient the system, someone still has to chop the onions.

Moral: The goal of kitchen strategy is not equilibrium — it's edible coexistence.

> **"Household Power Index 2025"**
>
> *The Institute for Domestic Economics reports that 61% of households identify the "primary cook" as the de facto head of decision-making. 49% admit to weaponizing food feedback as soft power. 12% describe mealtime as "open conflict with structured seating."*

Epilogue Fragment: The Leftover Clause

Tomorrow's peace is often built on tonight's leftovers — that quiet truce in Tupperware form. Because in the end, every great household learns the same truth: Power, like curry, tastes better reheated.

CHAPTER III

THE IN-LAW MATRIX: STAKEHOLDER MANAGEMENT, COALITION FORMATION, AND HOSTILE TAKEOVERS

Or: How to navigate cross-border alliances where love is local but politics is inherited.

I. The Situation

Every marriage begins with optimism, soft lighting, and Excel-level delusion. You think it's a merger — two people, one vision, unified assets. Then the **board of directors** arrives: parents, siblings, uncles, cousins, and that one aunt who doubles as the family's self-appointed Chief Emotional Auditor.

Suddenly, what looked like a clean M&A turns into a **multi-stakeholder integration**. Everyone claims to "want what's best," though "best" has 19 definitions and a WhatsApp group for each.

You don't just marry a person. You inherit a governance structure.

II. The Model: The In-Law Matrix

Borrowing from McKinsey's 2×2 obsession, we can visualize the In-Law ecosystem through **influence** (their power over your partner) and **alignment** (how much they actually like you).

	High Alignment	**Low Alignment**
High Influence	The Benevolent Dictator *("We love you, but call before decisions.")*	The Shadow Board *("We're just concerned. Deeply. Continuously.")*
Low Influence	The Cheerful Investor *("We trust you, dear. For now.")*	The Rogue Consultant *("Have you tried doing it the way we do it?")*

The goal, of course, is to move stakeholders diagonally — from **Shadow Board** to **Cheerful Investor** — without triggering regulatory scrutiny (also known as "family gossip").

III. Anecdotal Case Study: The Sunday Summit

Meet *Ananya and Rohan*, a couple whose love language is passive diplomacy.

Every Sunday, both sets of parents descend for what they call *"a casual meal."* What follows is an unmoderated shareholders' meeting.

Rohan's mother pushes for "traditional values." Ananya's father argues for "gender-neutral decision-making." Someone brings dessert and unsolicited advice. Everyone nods politely while strategizing revenge through WhatsApp forwards.

By dessert, peace is restored — temporarily. Both sides believe they've "won the conversation." In truth, no one remembers the issue. Only the score.

IV. The Behavioral Dynamics

In-laws operate on **relational power**, not formal authority. Their influence lies in emotional leverage, social optics, and the nuclear-grade weapon known as *the sigh.*

Psychologists refer to this as **familial signaling** — behaviors designed to remind you that love has conditional clauses.

Some classic tactics:

- **The Information Leak:** "We heard you're planning a vacation…" (They weren't told; they sensed it.)
- **The Advisory Coup:** "We're not interfering, just suggesting."
- **The Emotional Tender Offer:** "We just want you both to be happy — our way."

Each maneuver, though subtle, shifts the power equilibrium. What you mistake for small talk is, in fact, strategic positioning.

V. Archetypes in the In-Law Economy

Archetype	Core Strategy	Notable Behavior
The Silent Majority	Rules from the shadows	Uses relatives as proxies
The Corporate Aunt	Seeks consensus, enforces compliance	Runs the group chat like a PMO
The Perpetual Victim	Plays weak to remain powerful	Ends all calls with, "But don't worry about me."
The Benevolent Investor	Funds generously, audits emotionally	Believes ROI stands for *Return on Involvement*
The Political Outsourcer	"You deal with your side."	Treats love as bilateral treaty with redlines

🗨 *Margin note:* "Every family has a Ministry of Culture. It's usually one of your in-laws."

VI. The Strategic Framework: The In-Law Stakeholder Map

The **In-Law Stakeholder Map (ILSM)** identifies three operational goals:

1. **Containment:** Prevent minor interference from escalating into joint family ventures.
2. **Alignment:** Manage expectations through selective transparency.
3. **Diversification:** Cultivate multiple informal allies for redundancy in crises.

Visually, imagine a network diagram with you at the center, arrows pointing outward. Green arrows indicate "safe alliances," yellow ones "conditional tolerance," and red ones "permanent oversight."

The mature strategist aims not to eliminate the reds, but to **redirect them toward each other.**

That's coalition politics, family edition.

VII. Anecdotal Addendum: The Festival Wars

Nothing tests stakeholder alignment like holidays. Each festival becomes an annual summit, complete with agenda: *"Whose house this year?"*

The wrong answer can destabilize quarters of goodwill. A single misplaced visit order (his side before hers) can trigger emotional recession. The recovery period averages 3–5 business days, depending on quality of apology and dessert provided.

The lesson: manage expectations like a budget. Never promise equal time; promise **equally plausible excuses.**

VIII. The Corporate Parallel

In-law management is corporate stakeholder theory in its purest form — high emotion, low data, and infinite review cycles.

- **The Mother-in-law:** Legacy stakeholder — resists change but owns most of the emotional equity.
- **The Father-in-law:** Institutional investor — detached until liquidity (grandchildren) arrives.
- **Siblings:** Competing startups — agile, disruptive, emotionally volatile.
- **Cousins:** Lateral hires — unnecessary but politically significant.

Just as companies balance activist shareholders, couples balance *activist families*: entities convinced they understand your business model better than you do.

The seasoned executive doesn't fight the board; they learn to redirect it.

IX. The Existential Undercurrent

The family, for all its complexity, is the original network organization — no bylaws, no exits, infinite feedback loops. The in-laws are simply middle management between you and the gods of tradition.

Their interference, though maddening, is also proof of belonging. Indifference would be far worse.

So, you learn to smile, nod, and practice selective hearing — the ancient art of strategic ignorance. Because every relationship needs friction to stay warm; the trick is not to let it ignite.

X. The Moral (Filed and Archived)

Stakeholder harmony isn't achieved through transparency — it's maintained through *curated opacity.*

Moral: The key to managing in-laws, like investors, is to make them believe they're shaping decisions you've already made.

> **"The Family Governance Index (FGI) 2025"**
>
> *A study by the Institute for Applied Domestic Strategy found that 68% of couples report "stakeholder interference" in key life decisions, 27% have considered "offsite conflict resolution" (vacationing separately), and 5% admit to running separate budget sheets labeled "parent-friendly narratives."*

Epilogue Fragment: The Post-Dinner Debrief

Every couple, after the relatives leave, conducts the same closed-door audit:

"Did that go well?" "Depends who you ask."

And so, the household survives another fiscal quarter — love intact, nerves frayed, and the board ever watchful.

CHAPTER IV

THE WEEKEND PROJECT FALLACY: THE SUNK COST TRAP AND OVER-OPTIMISM BIAS IN HOME REPAIRS

> *Or: Why every do-it-yourself initiative eventually becomes an exercise in self-discovery and mild despair.*

I. The Situation

It begins with optimism — the most dangerous of human resources.

Saturday morning. You're holding a screwdriver, watching a YouTube tutorial titled *"Fix Anything in 5 Minutes!"* The man in the video wears confidence like a uniform. He says things like, "It's really simple once you understand the mechanism."

You nod sagely. You have never understood a mechanism in your life, but you believe in learning by breaking.

Fast forward three hours: You're surrounded by washers, screws, and existential dread. The tap is still leaking — now proudly in *two* directions. You whisper, "Almost there," because admitting defeat would mean acknowledging sunk cost.

The weekend project is no longer a task. It's a metaphor for the human condition.

II. The Model: The Home Repair Sunk Cost Loop

In economics, the **Sunk Cost Fallacy** is the tendency to continue an endeavor purely because of what's already been invested — time, money, ego.

In domestic strategy, it manifests as:

"I've already bought the tools, might as well finish the job."

The loop looks like this:

Initial Confidence → Minor Setback → Increased Commitment → Catastrophic Error → Existential Rationalization

At this point, your project transitions from "improvement" to "reconstruction." You are not fixing a pipe; you are protecting your self-esteem.

III. Anecdotal Case Study: The Shelf of Denial

Take *Aditya*, who once decided to "save money" by installing floating bookshelves. He purchased the finest tools, watched tutorials, even used phrases like "load-bearing wall."

Five hours later, the shelf was up — slightly diagonal, spiritually exhausted. He stepped back, admired his work, and thought, *"Not bad."*

The next morning, gravity held a board meeting. By noon, the shelf had resigned from its position. Aditya now calls the scar on his wall "a minimalist installation."

IV. The Behavioral Breakdown

Home projects seduce us because they flatter our illusion of agency. They whisper: *You are capable, self-sufficient, and one hex key away from mastery.*

But the real bias isn't optimism — it's **competence delusion.**

Cognitive psychologists refer to this as the **Dunning–Do-It-Yourself Effect:**

The less you know, the more YouTube makes you feel invincible.

Other forces at play:

- **Planning Fallacy:** Every repair seems like "a quick job." Reality runs on geological time.
- **Escalation of Commitment:** Once you've made one hole in the wall, you'll make ten more to justify it.
- **Illusion of Progress:** The more mess you create, the more convinced you are that work is happening.

The modern homeowner's mantra: *"It looks worse, but it's getting better."*

V. Archetypes of the Weekend Strategist

Archetype	Core Strategy	Common Failure Mode
The Tool Collector	Buys specialized gadgets for every task	Forgets what half of them do
The Overconfident Minimalist	"All I need is duct tape."	All they have is duct tape
The Perfectionist	Redoes everything thrice	Finishes nothing
The Improviser	Uses butter knives as screwdrivers	Writes poems about futility
The Delegation Convert	Calls a plumber after breaking everything	Describes it later as "a joint effort"

🗨 *Margin note:* "Every DIY project ends with the phrase: 'Next time, I'll plan better.' There is no next time."

VI. The Strategic Takeaway: Managing the Domestic Sunk Cost Curve

The **Domestic Sunk Cost Curve (DSCC)** can be expressed as:

$$\textit{Satisfaction} = \textit{Initial Vision} - (\textit{Effort}^2 \times \textit{Error})$$

Meaning: enthusiasm decays exponentially with time, while regret compounds hourly.

The professional strategist knows when to pivot; the amateur homeowner knows when to double down. To escape the loop, apply the **90-Minute Rule**:

If you're still optimistic after 90 minutes, stop immediately. You're delusional.

The true victory in home repair lies not in completion, but in knowing when to outsource.

VII. Anecdote Two: The Great Paint Disaster

When *Ritika and Karan* decided to "paint the bedroom themselves," it began as couple bonding. Two hours in, Karan was quoting TED Talks about teamwork; Ritika was researching annulment.

The wall ended up looking like postmodern art. They called it *"Texture."* Visitors politely called it *"bold."* Their landlord called it *"unacceptable."*

They paid a painter to fix it — for twice the cost. But when asked, they said, *"We learned a lot."* Which, in behavioral finance terms, translates to: **non-refundable enlightenment.**

VIII. The Corporate Parallel

Corporations suffer the same disease under fancier names. They pour millions into doomed projects because *"we've already invested too much to stop."* They hold meetings about "strategic patience," which is corporate code for "we have no idea what we're doing, but we've done it too long to quit."

Just like the weekend handyman, the corporate executive finds comfort in continuity. It's not logic — it's inertia wearing a tie.

The difference is that corporations write off sunk costs; homeowners write them into dinner-table anecdotes.

IX. The Existential Undercurrent

The impulse to fix things ourselves is noble — even tender. It's proof we still believe the world can be improved through willpower and manual effort. That our hands, however untrained, can wrestle entropy into submission.

But maybe the wiser act isn't fixing — it's accepting. Maybe the true craft lies in knowing which leaks to live with.

In the end, every loose screw is just a reminder: perfection was never part of the floor plan.

X. The Moral (Hand-Sanded and Slightly Uneven)

All repairs are autobiographical. We patch walls the way we patch ourselves — imperfectly, defiantly, hoping no one notices the seams.

Moral: Strategy isn't knowing how to fix everything; it's knowing what can stay broken without ruining dinner.

"Domestic Overconfidence Index 2025"

Study by the Institute of Behavioral Home Economics: 82% of DIY enthusiasts underestimate project duration by at least 60%. 64% sustain "non-medical injuries." 47% say they'd "absolutely do it again." Economists classify this behavior under **Chronic Hopefulness Disorder (CHD).**

Epilogue Fragment: The Sunday Audit

Sunday evening. You survey your creation — half-done, oddly personal, quietly resilient. It wobbles, yes. But so do you.

You close your toolbox, whisper to yourself:

"It's not perfect, but it's mine."

And that, really, is the most efficient cost–benefit outcome you'll ever get at home.

CHAPTER V

SIBLING RIVALRY AS MARKET SEGMENTATION

> *Or: How the same parents produce two entirely different brands fighting for the same customer.*

I. The Situation

Every family begins as a monopoly. The first child arrives, cornering 100 percent of the parental attention market. Then one day—usually right after the first starts sleeping through the night—management decides to "expand capacity."

Enter Competitor #2: smaller, louder, and backed by aggressive investor sentiment.

What follows is not a family drama. It's a live-action MBA case on **resource allocation under scarcity**. Every bedtime story, every exam report, every extra slice of cake becomes a quarterly performance metric.

The parents call it *"love."* The children call it *"unfair."* Economists call it *"natural selection with emotional paperwork."*

II. The Model: Differentiation and Strategic Positioning

In markets with limited demand (affection, praise, Wi-Fi bandwidth), players must differentiate to survive.

Strategy	Typical Child Behavior	Market Outcome
Cost Leadership	Does chores without complaint	Wins reliability contracts
Differentiation	Becomes artistic / gifted	Captures niche admiration
Focus Strategy	Specializes in one parental weakness	Monopolizes that vertical ("Dad's Favourite")
Disruption	Cries loudly, innovates chaos	Forces regime change

The family thus evolves into a **miniature oligopoly**, each child protecting market share through narrative branding:

"I'm the responsible one." "I'm the creative one." "I'm adopted, probably."

III. Anecdotal Case Study: The Exam Wars

Consider *Megha* (14) and *Rohit* (12). Same parents, same school, different public-relations departments.

After every exam, their living room becomes an investor briefing. Megha presents her report calmly, highlighting consistency and long-term potential. Rohit interrupts with "I got extra marks for handwriting!" — a classic **short-term market signal**.

The mother, torn between ROI and emotional diversification, says,

"You're both doing well in your own ways."

Translation: *the firm remains profitable, but margins are tightening.*

IV. The Behavioral Dynamics

Sibling rivalry thrives on two biases:

1. **Relative Utility:** Satisfaction is measured not by what you have, but by how much more you have than your sibling.
2. **Loss Aversion:** Praise feels good, but hearing "your brother got 98" feels like bankruptcy.

Psychologists call this **The Comparison Trap**; strategists call it **Benchmark Competition**. Both lead to one predictable outcome — chronic under-celebration.

V. Archetypes in the Household Market

Archetype	Core Tactic	Hidden Weakness
The Elder Conglomerate	Relies on legacy goodwill	Declining innovation
The Younger Disruptor	Uses agility and cuteness	Short attention span
The Middle Subsidiary	Diversifies quietly	Perpetual identity crisis
The Black-Sheep Startup	Rejects the whole system	Needs new investors
The Joint Venture Pair	Temporary sibling alliance	Collapses post-dessert

🗨 *Margin note:* "Family IPO rule: when one child goes public with achievement, the other files a grievance."

VI. Strategic Takeaway: The Household Portfolio Effect

Parents manage risk like fund managers — balancing over-performers and under-performers to maintain emotional diversification. This yields the **Household Portfolio Effect (HPE):**

Total family harmony ≈ Inverse of Attention Volatility × Snack Availability

The optimal equilibrium isn't equality; it's **rotational favoritism.** Each child gets a temporary bull run in affection before the market corrects.

Smart siblings learn *co-opetition*:

- Collaborate during external crises (exams, guests).
- Compete internally for bonus allocations (extra screen time).

VII. Anecdote Two: The Inheritance Simulation

When their parents bought one bicycle, *Ravi* and *Anu* agreed to "share." By week two, Ravi had implemented a **ride-time quota system** with performance metrics ("laps per hour"). Anu retaliated with **regulatory complaints** ("Mom! He's monopolizing!").

The parents intervened by buying a second bicycle. Peace returned — until Ravi upgraded his seat. Anu demanded *parity adjustment.* Economists recorded it as a **proportional-envy spiral**.

VIII. The Corporate Parallel

Companies mirror families more than they admit. Business units fight for budget. Teams hoard data. CEOs declare "we're one big family," unaware they're describing the problem, not the solution.

In both systems:

- Collaboration is seasonal.
- Loyalty is conditional.
- Recognition is a finite resource distributed through inconsistent appraisals.

The only difference? In families, the board never retires; it just gets louder during festivals.

IX. The Existential Undercurrent

Sibling rivalry endures because it serves a purpose — it gives shape to identity. Without contrast, who would we be?

We define ourselves against our nearest competitor, then spend adulthood pretending we've moved past it. But the truth leaks out every time someone says, "Mom still likes you best."

What begins as competition for toys evolves into competition for validation — and eventually, into affection disguised as sarcasm.

X. The Moral (Framed in the Family Photo)

Every sibling war is a training program for adult diplomacy. We learn negotiation, empathy, and the art of pretending not to care who got the bigger piece.

Moral: The smartest strategy isn't winning the household market; it's staying solvent enough to laugh about it later.

"Sibling Equity Index (2025)"

Institute of Domestic Behavioral Economics findings: – 89 % of adults admit to believing their parents "had a favorite." – 73 % claim they were that favorite. – Mathematically, 62 % are delusional.

Epilogue Fragment: The Annual Home Reunion

The children grow up, move out, and diversify portfolios. Yet every festival dinner still reopens the market. Old rivalries flicker alive between servings of dessert. Because family, like capitalism, never truly ends — it just goes into generational restructuring.

CHAPTER VI

PARENTING AS CHANGE MANAGEMENT

> *Or: Why every bedtime routine is a failed corporate transformation plan.*

I. The Situation

The parenting journey begins like an ambitious transformation program. You have a *vision statement* ("We'll raise independent thinkers"), a *mission plan* ("Screen-free playtime"), and a *project sponsor* ("Grandparents, intermittently").

For the first few months, everything seems aligned. The baby sleeps. You post thought leadership on Instagram. Then the baby learns to say "no."

Congratulations — your household has entered the **Resistance Phase.**

From this point on, parenting is a real-time MBA in stakeholder management, expectation calibration, and crisis PR. The only measurable KPI is survival, and even that is subject to revision during adolescence.

II. The Model: Kotter's 8 Steps for Domestic Transformation

John Kotter, the management guru, proposed an 8-step framework for driving change. Applied to parenting, it becomes less about "visionary leadership" and more about "negotiating with tiny union leaders."

Kotter Step	Parenting Translation	Typical Outcome
1. Create urgency	"Because I said so!"	Immediate pushback
2. Build a guiding coalition	"Ask your mother."	Internal misalignment
3. Form a strategic vision	"No screens before dinner."	Vision decay by Tuesday
4. Enlist volunteers	"Who wants to help fold clothes?"	Silence
5. Enable action	Bribes disguised as encouragement	Temporary compliance
6. Generate short-term wins	"Good job!" for basic hygiene	Inflated self-esteem index
7. Sustain acceleration	Repeat until exhausted	Parental burnout
8. Anchor new approaches	"This is the new rule."	Rebellion by bedtime

Parenting is thus a perpetual turnaround — change initiatives launched every morning, quietly abandoned by dusk.

III. Anecdotal Case Study: The Great Bedtime Reform

Take *Neha and Arjun*, idealistic parents who once decided to "establish structure."

They introduced a new **Bedtime Policy Framework (v1.0)** — dinner by 8, brushing by 8:30, lights out by 9. They even held a *kickoff meeting* with their 6-year-old stakeholder, complete with vision slides ("Better sleep = happier mornings!").

Night one went well. Night two ended in negotiations ("Two stories, not one"). By night four, the child had unionized, demanding higher compensation (extra cartoon time). By night five, the policy had been "temporarily suspended pending review."

They called it *flexibility.* Consultants call it *scope creep.*

IV. The Behavioral Dynamics

Children resist change for the same reason adults do — **loss of autonomy**. What feels like structure to you feels like oppression to them.

Psychologists call this **psychological reactance** — the impulse to do the opposite of what one's told, simply to prove free will exists.

Parents, in turn, develop **illusion of control bias** — the belief that carefully worded instructions can override evolutionary chaos. They confuse *communication* with *compliance.*

The result: a household that runs on **adaptive improvisation**, powered by coffee and guilt.

V. Archetypes of Parental Strategy

Archetype	Core Strategy	Failure Mode
The Visionary Leader	"We'll raise global citizens."	Ends up negotiating curfews
The Benevolent Manager	"Let's talk about your feelings."	Gets overthrown by emotions
The Authoritarian CEO	"Because I said so."	Employee attrition (emotional)
The Agile Parent	"We're learning together."	Rebrands confusion as mindfulness

Archetype	Core Strategy	Failure Mode
The Outsourcer	"Your aunt will handle this."	Outsources both authority and blame

🗨 *Margin note:* "Children don't need structure. They are structure — disorder disguised as growth."

VI. The Strategic Takeaway: The Home as a Living System

The core insight: **Parenting isn't change management. It's chaos stewardship.**

Corporate change assumes rational actors, stable hierarchies, and measurable outcomes. Parenting offers none of those luxuries. Instead, it teaches **complex adaptive strategy** — incremental adjustments based on daily behavioral feedback.

The secret isn't control, but *co-evolution.* You don't manage change; you change together, clumsily and repeatedly, until habit feels like harmony.

In systems terms:

Stability = Function (Flexibility × Emotional Recovery Speed)

The faster you forgive yesterday's disaster, the more tomorrow feels like progress.

VII. Anecdote Two: The Homework Transformation Program

When *Amit* decided to "empower" his daughter to manage her homework, he implemented a **Task Ownership Framework** — colorful charts, motivational stickers, accountability checkpoints.

For one week, it worked. Then she outsourced accountability back to him, claiming "strategic overwhelm." He rebranded the failure as "a learning sprint."

Eventually, they reached equilibrium: she did half the work, he did half the worrying. In consulting terms, this was declared *successfully transitioned to steady state operations.*

VIII. The Corporate Parallel

Workplaces love to borrow the language of parenting — *nurture talent, create safe spaces, build growth mindsets.* But it's really the other way around: parenting borrows the pretense of business.

Every parent runs a micro-enterprise of unpredictable stakeholders. Every child is both employee and customer — entitled, demanding, un-fireable.

Like most organizations, families survive not by clarity of vision, but by endurance of ambiguity. And like most corporate transformations, parenting delivers the one outcome consultants never predict: **love, despite metrics.**

IX. The Existential Undercurrent

Perhaps the reason parenting feels like failure is that it's meant to. You're managing yourself out of obsolescence. The better you do your job, the less relevant you become.

Children grow up, systems mature, and the house once full of noise becomes eerily compliant.

That silence — which once felt like success — now feels like loss disguised as efficiency.

Maybe the goal was never "change management." Maybe it was simply *to stay changed yourself.*

X. The Moral (Still Awake at 11:30 p.m.)

Parenting is the only project where losing control gracefully counts as mastery.

Moral: The secret of domestic strategy is knowing when to stop leading and start listening — preferably before someone throws a toy.

"Parental Change Index (PCI) 2025"

Institute for Domestic Transformation Studies data: – 94% of parents admit to abandoning at least one rule "for peace." – 73% claim their children "don't take them seriously." – 28% say they "now identify as facilitators." Economists classify parenting as a **perpetual restructuring process with infinite goodwill write-offs.**

Epilogue Fragment: The Morning After

You wake up to chaos: socks missing, breakfast burning, arguments over cereal brands. You sigh, reset the system, and relaunch the day's transformation plan.

The child looks up and says, "Can we do it my way?" You smile. "We already are."

ARC II: MICRO-MOVES, MACRO-GAINS

STRATEGY IN THE MUNDANE

CHAPTER VII

THE GREAT COMMUTE GAME: REAL OPTIONS THEORY MEETS TRAFFIC NAVIGATION

> *Or: How every morning is an MBA in uncertainty management.*

I. The Situation

It begins the same way every weekday: the alarm goes off, you negotiate with your future self, and lose.

Outside, the city hums like a bad mood warming up. You glance at Google Maps — a kaleidoscope of red lines that look suspiciously like capillaries under stress. You whisper, *"Maybe it'll clear up."* It never does.

Thus begins the modern gladiatorial ritual known as **The Commute** — a recurring case study in risk assessment, cognitive bias, and mild existential despair.

You aren't just travelling; you're performing **live operations research** with bad coffee.

II. The Model: Real Options Theory (ROT) for the Rest of Us

In finance, *Real Options Theory* says it's valuable to delay decisions until uncertainty resolves. In traffic, this translates to:

"Maybe if I leave ten minutes later, things will magically improve."

Spoiler: they won't. But the **illusion of flexibility** keeps us sane.

Option	Description	Expected Payoff	Hidden Cost
Early Departure Call Option	Leave absurdly early to "beat traffic."	Arrive on time, resent the world.	Lose sleep, dignity.
Flexible Delay Option	Wait for conditions to "normalize."	None.	Everything worsens by 15 minutes.
Route Switch Option	Experiment with side roads.	Occasional triumph.	Statistical heartbreak.
Modal Hedge Option	Try metro, bus, or ride-share.	Variable returns, social exposure.	Contamination by humanity.

The successful commuter isn't the fastest; they're the least disappointed.

III. Anecdotal Case Study: The Three-Route Fallacy

Meet *Pranav*, a mid-level consultant whose true calling is traffic analytics.

Every morning he toggles between three possible routes: A (shortest distance), B (fewer signals), and C ("just vibes"). He records travel times in an Excel sheet labeled *Mobility Optimization Dashboard v5.0.*

After six months of data collection, he concludes that average arrival time is **identical across all routes**. He publishes a report titled *"The Inevitability of Gridlock."* His manager calls it "depressing but insightful."

Behavioral takeaway: information seldom improves outcomes, only narratives.

IV. The Behavioral Dynamics

Traffic transforms rational humans into stochastic variables. Inside a car, people oscillate between **illusory control** ("If I honk, they'll move") and **learned helplessness** ("Let the universe decide").

Economists describe commuting as *pure deadweight loss* — time irretrievably spent doing nothing productive. Psychologists disagree: it's *emotional cross-training.*

Biases at play:

- **Optimism Bias:** "Tomorrow will be lighter." It won't.
- **Control Illusion:** "I choose the lane." The lane chooses you.
- **Social Proof:** Following others into a jam because they seem confident.
- **Endowment Effect:** Defending "your lane" as if you own it.

In short, the road is just a mirror with tail-lights.

V. Archetypes of the Commuter Ecosystem

Archetype	Core Strategy	Distinguishing Behavior
The Spreadsheet Strategist	Logs departure times	Publishes quarterly findings no one reads

Archetype	Core Strategy	Distinguishing Behavior
The Zen Driver	Accepts fate	Listens to podcasts on acceptance while swearing softly
The Aggressive Optimizer	Overtakes in 2 metres	Loses faith in humanity hourly
The Ride-Share Skeptic	Joins for efficiency	Leaves for sanity
The Public-Transport Stoic	Lives by schedule	Knows true patience is not a virtue but a necessity

Margin note: "Every honk is a KPI for emotional volatility."

VI. The Strategic Takeaway: The Option Value of Acceptance

In finance, holding an option lets you benefit from volatility. In commuting, the only valuable option is **emotional hedging** — cultivating indifference.

The **Commute Utility Curve** looks like this:

Satisfaction = Arrival Time × (1 / Expectation)

Lower expectations raise returns. Hence, the wisest travelers expect nothing — and are rarely disappointed.

The real strategy is *adaptive routing*: micro-pivots in attitude, not asphalt.

VII. Anecdote Two: The Corporate Commute Hack

When Riya's company introduced flexible hours, she rejoiced — "Now I'll skip traffic!" Within weeks, everyone had the same idea. Traffic merely shifted forward by one hour.

Riya realized she hadn't escaped the system; she'd moved its boundaries. She now leaves whenever she feels like it — and accepts whatever happens. Her commute time remains unchanged. Her blood pressure does not.

She calls it "strategic surrender." Consultants call it "wisdom."

VIII. The Corporate Parallel

Corporations commute too — between strategies, visions, and reorgs. Each new initiative promises efficiency; each ends in gridlock of committees. The executives blame "external factors." The real issue is lane-discipline.

A CEO stuck in decision traffic resembles a driver at a blocked signal: impatient, self-righteous, and secretly aware that everyone else is too.

In both cases, progress arrives only when someone accepts stagnation gracefully.

IX. The Existential Undercurrent

The commute is our daily pilgrimage to powerlessness. It reminds us that no matter how carefully we plan, we move at the city's pace.

Some find rage; others find rhythm. Those who learn to float within the jam — neither rushing nor resisting — achieve the rare state of **transcendental idling.**

The engine hums, time melts, and you realize: the destination was just an excuse to begin.

X. The Moral (Still in Traffic)

Commuting isn't a waste of time. It's a course in humility taught daily at rush hour.

Moral: Strategic calm outperforms tactical speed — especially when no one's moving.

"Urban Mobility Index 2025"

Institute for Applied Everyday Strategy findings: – Average urban commuter spends 84 minutes daily in traffic. – 39 % track alternate routes they never use. – 61 % believe honking "creates momentum." Economists classify commuting as a **predictable loss disguised as participation.**

Epilogue Fragment: The Late Arrival

You finally reach work. Your boss says, "Rough traffic?" You nod — the universal corporate alibi for existential delay.

He smiles, late for his next meeting. You smile too, late for nothing in particular. Outside, the city continues its slow, beautiful jam.

CHAPTER VIII

QUEUE THEORY AND SUPERMARKET STRATEGY

> *Or: Why the other line is always faster — and what that says about your soul.*

I. The Situation

There comes a moment in every grocery run when you must choose. You've gathered your produce, out-maneuvered a trolley traffic jam, and arrived at the **Final Frontier**: the checkout lines.

You scan them like a general before battle — assessing cart volume, scanning-speed of cashiers, and the suspicious aura of coupon clippers. You pick a line confidently, guided by intuition and irrational hope.

Two minutes later, the other line moves first.

A familiar heat spreads through your chest — part injustice, part jealousy, part philosophy. You realize you're not buying groceries anymore; you're buying **an experiment in probability and regret.**

II. The Model: Basic Queueing Theory (as Misapplied by Civilians)

Classical **Queueing Theory** studies how systems manage waiting — customers arrive, are served, and depart. Supermarkets are its perfect (and cruel) laboratory.

In theory, average wait time = $\lambda / (\mu - \lambda)$, where λ is arrival rate and μ is service rate. In reality, average wait time = *How fast the line you didn't pick moves.*

Concept	Real-World Interpretation	Emotional Effect
Arrival Rate (λ)	People materializing the moment you switch lines	Panic
Service Rate (μ)	Cashier's scanning speed × competence × mood	Denial
Queue Discipline	"First-come, first-served" (theory) → "First-loud, first-served" (practice)	Fury
Utilization	How close system is to collapse	99 % (always)

The problem isn't math — it's **psychological asymmetry**: we notice every delay in our line but not the equivalent pauses in others.

III. Anecdotal Case Study: The Checkout Betrayal

Meet *Suresh*, a man with a PhD in Overthinking. He once committed to Line 3, drawn by a single shopper holding only "a few things."

That shopper then produced a shopping list longer than *War and Peace*, plus a loyalty card that needed "reactivation." Meanwhile, Line 4 surged ahead — led by a grandmother paying entirely in cash, effortlessly efficient.

By the time Suresh reached the register, he'd developed a 40-slide internal presentation titled *"Operational Inefficiencies in Retail Queue Dynamics."* He never published it. He just muttered it weekly.

IV. The Behavioral Dynamics

Waiting is agony because it weaponizes **uncertainty**. Our brains are bad at boredom but worse at helplessness.

Psychologists identify three culprits:

1. **Temporal Myopia:** We overestimate how long we've waited once frustration begins.
2. **Illusion of Control:** Switching lines feels like action, even when counter-productive.
3. **Outcome Bias:** We remember the one time switching helped — and forget the dozen it didn't.

Thus emerges the **Queue Paradox:**

The longer you deliberate, the less likely your decision will satisfy you — yet the more confident you'll remain that you "almost beat the system."

V. Archetypes in the Supermarket Ecosystem

Archetype	Core Strategy	Typical Behavior
The Lane Analyst	Studies queue length × basket size	Misses opening of new counter
The Impatient Arbitrageur	Switches lines frequently	Loses position and dignity
The Loyal Liner	Stays put, suffers silently	Gains moral superiority points

Archetype	Core Strategy	Typical Behavior
The Social Opportunist	Strikes up conversation	Converts strangers into allies or enemies
The Self-Checkout Evangelist	"Technology will save us"	Argues with scanner for eternity

🗨 *Margin note:* "Patience is just inefficiency with good PR."

VI. The Strategic Takeaway: The Myth of Efficiency

The **Expected Utility of Switching (EUS)** can be summarized as:

EUS = (Perceived Gain × Hope) – (Actual Time Lost × Shame)

In all known experiments, **EUS < 0.** Translation: staying put is statistically wiser, emotionally harder.

Therefore, the optimal supermarket strategy is **informed inertia** — choose once, then surrender completely. Progress is often just peace disguised as waiting.

VII. Anecdote Two: The Express-Lane Illusion

Priya, chronically late yet spiritually ambitious, once spotted a new "10 items or fewer" lane. She raced there triumphantly, clutching exactly 10 items.

The person ahead had 11. The cashier insisted on principle. An argument broke out that froze all other counters.

Priya stood motionless, watching time evaporate, and whispered the modern mantra:

"I should've just stayed where I was."

And that, dear reader, is what enlightenment sounds like in aisle 7.

VIII. The Corporate Parallel

Office life runs on queues — approvals, sign-offs, IT tickets, promotions. Each department believes it's the "express lane." Every individual suspects they're in the wrong one.

Executives propose automation. HR proposes empathy. Both lengthen the queue. The employee who endures without expectation eventually discovers the corporate equivalent of serenity: *calendar resignation.*

IX. The Existential Undercurrent

All waiting is a rehearsal for mortality — proof that time moves even when we don't. We fill it with scrolling, sighing, or moral superiority, but underneath lies the same realization:

No one truly knows when it'll be their turn.

Perhaps that's why supermarket queues feel spiritual — tiny reminders that fairness exists mostly as policy signage.

X. The Moral (Still at Checkout)

Efficiency is overrated. Acceptance clears faster.

Moral: The wiser strategist optimizes not for time saved, but for peace preserved.

"National Queue Sentiment Survey 2025"

Institute for Everyday Systems reports: – 87 % of shoppers believe their line moved slower. – 46 % switched lanes; 92 % regretted it. – 12 % found unexpected joy talking to strangers. Economists define this phenomenon as **Negative Throughput with Positive Character Development.**

Epilogue Fragment: The Parking-Lot Epiphany

Outside, bags in hand, you see the same cashier closing another line — your old one. For a fleeting moment, you feel both foolish and free.

The car keys jingle. The world resumes. And you think: *Next time, I'll plan better.* You won't — but you'll believe you will.

CHAPTER IX

THE UMBRELLA HEDGE FUND

> *Or: Risk mitigation and decision trees under weather uncertainty.*

I. The Situation

Morning. You look out the window — the sky is a moody grey, not quite threatening, not quite trustworthy.

The weather app says "20% chance of rain." You stare at it, as if squinting might reveal what that 20% actually means.

You ask yourself the question that has humbled philosophers, executives, and interns alike:

"Should I take the umbrella?"

It's never really about the umbrella. It's about your appetite for regret.

Because if you take it, it won't rain. If you don't, it will. And thus, the universe quietly mocks your every attempt at probabilistic reasoning.

II. The Model: The Umbrella Decision Tree

The classical **Decision Tree** applies perfectly here: a simple two-branch model leading inevitably to disappointment.

Decision	Outcome	Emotional Return
Take umbrella	It rains	Smug satisfaction (+5)

Decision	Outcome	Emotional Return
Take umbrella	It doesn't rain	Carrying dead weight, mild shame (–3)
Don't take umbrella	It rains	Existential humiliation (–10)
Don't take umbrella	It doesn't rain	False sense of genius (+3)

From this, we derive the **Expected Utility of Preparedness (EUP)**:

EUP = (Probability of Rain × Relief) – (Probability of Dryness × Burden)

The optimal strategy? Always carry the umbrella. The optimal human response? Never learn.

III. Anecdotal Case Study: The Office Hero

Take *Rahul*, a man of conviction and permanently wet socks. Every morning he tells himself, *"It won't rain today. I'm manifesting sunshine."* He mocks colleagues carrying umbrellas as "risk-averse conformists."

By evening, he's sheltering under a tea stall, recalculating the **Value at Rain (VaR)** of his decision. He swears next time he'll bring one. Next time, of course, it doesn't rain. Rahul's been oscillating between smugness and pneumonia since 2017.

IV. The Behavioral Dynamics

The umbrella dilemma activates our deepest cognitive biases:

- **Optimism Bias:** "It won't happen to me." (It will.)
- **Loss Aversion:** The pain of looking foolish with a dry umbrella outweighs the joy of staying dry in rain.

- **Outcome Blindness:** We remember the times we carried it needlessly, not the times it saved us.

In short, we aren't managing weather — we're managing embarrassment.

This is known in behavioral finance as **the Regret Minimization Portfolio.** We diversify not against risk, but against ridicule.

V. Archetypes of Weather Strategy

Archetype	Core Philosophy	Typical Outcome
The Rational Hedger	"Always be covered."	Overprepared, slightly smug
The Naked Optimist	"It'll clear up."	Drenched, unrepentant
The Data Scientist	Checks 4 apps	Confused by conflicting APIs
The Opportunist	Borrows umbrellas	Avoids risk, cultivates resentment
The Existential Minimalist	"We're all wet, metaphorically."	Accepts fate, never late

🗨 *Margin note:* "Forecasts are the corporate version of prayers — public, vague, and wrong half the time."

VI. The Strategic Takeaway: The Hedge Principle

The **Umbrella Hedge Fund (UHF)** operates on one key principle:

A small inconvenience today prevents large-scale soaking tomorrow.

Translated into finance: – The umbrella = insurance premium. – The rain = market volatility. – You = perpetually underdiversified investor.

Yet humans routinely underinsure against predictable discomfort. We'd rather gamble on luck than carry proof of caution. Because being wrong optimistically feels better than being right pessimistically.

That, in essence, is the emotional core of capitalism — and of umbrellas.

VII. Anecdote Two: The Shared Umbrella Joint Venture

During monsoon, *Nisha* and *Kartik* shared one umbrella — a 50–50 partnership based on mutual trust and poor spatial planning. At first, it was romantic. Then came logistical friction: unequal coverage, strategic shoulder exposure, and the infamous *drip arbitration.*

By week two, the partnership dissolved amid accusations of "umbrella hogging." Both reverted to independent hedging. In interviews, they described the breakup as "an amicable liquidation."

VIII. The Corporate Parallel

Corporate risk managers and commuters share the same pathology — the illusion that prediction equals control. Companies buy insurance but ignore preparation. They invest in forecasting tools that produce PDFs, not foresight.

Every annual report mentions "unpredictable macroeconomic conditions" — the business equivalent of "partly cloudy." And every CEO insists, "We'll be ready next time." They won't. But they'll issue a strongly worded weather statement.

IX. The Existential Undercurrent

Rain is democracy in liquid form. It humbles everyone — the rich, the punctual, the self-assured. It reminds us that planning is performative; adaptation is real.

Carrying an umbrella won't stop the rain, but it declares faith in *preparedness over prophecy.* It's a small, foldable act of defiance against chaos — a handle on uncertainty.

X. The Moral (Still Dripping)

We can't predict the rain, only the regret. The wise traveler chooses the lighter burden.

Moral: Carry the umbrella — not because you'll need it, but because someday you'll thank yourself for hoping you might.

"Rain Probability Sentiment Index (2025)"

Institute for Applied Uncertainty Studies reports: – 78% of urban commuters carry umbrellas "only if others do." – 61% believe the act itself influences rainfall (magical thinking). – 34% lose their umbrellas within one week of purchase. Economists classify this under **Behavioral Leakages.**

Epilogue Fragment: The Damp Redemption

It rains just enough to make your decision meaningful. You open the umbrella, feeling both clever and mortal.

Beside you, someone drenched mutters, "Lucky day." You smile. It wasn't luck. It was learned pessimism — the only reliable forecast there is.

CHAPTER X

PUBLIC TRANSPORT AS A LESSON IN SYSTEMS THINKING

Or: Bottlenecks, buffers, and the fragile supply chain of human patience.

I. The Situation

Morning rush hour. The bus stop hums with optimism and carbon dioxide.

A small crowd assembles, each commuter performing their preferred ritual of waiting:

- The Hopeful Peerer (craning for the bus that isn't yet visible).
- The Timetable Believer (checking an app that hasn't been updated since 2018).
- The Fatalist (already resigned, emotionally boarded).

Then, in the distance — movement! The bus appears, magnificent and full. You prepare your strategy: approach vector, door proximity, and subtle elbow deployment.

When it finally halts, it's already full of other strategists. You step in anyway, violating both physics and self-respect.

And so begins the daily group simulation known as **Urban Systems Failure in Real Time.**

II. The Model: Systems Thinking in Motion (and Mostly, Not)

Systems Thinking, as taught to engineers and business schools, tells us that complex systems are not linear — they're cyclical, adaptive, and governed by feedback loops. Public transport proves this daily.

Let's break down the ecosystem:

System Component	Example in Transit	Behavioral Analogue
Input Flow	Passengers arriving faster than the schedule allows	Demand spike
Processing Rate	Bus capacity × conductor tolerance	System throughput
Buffer	Standing room and the driver's optimism	Temporary elasticity
Bottleneck	The one narrow door	Lifetime metaphor
Feedback Loop	Angry commuters delaying departure further	Self-reinforcing inefficiency

This is the **Law of Commuter Thermodynamics:**

In any enclosed public system, irritation will always increase unless acted upon by an external apology.

III. Anecdotal Case Study: The Great Metro Bottleneck

Consider *Meenakshi*, a regular metro commuter whose morning routine is synchronized with the 8:17 train. On good days, she gets a seat. On average days, she gets a pole. On bad days, she becomes the pole.

One morning, a minor delay caused a **queue compaction cascade** — each passenger pressed slightly closer to the next until the train resembled a human data archive. When the driver announced “technical hold,” time froze. Meenakshi found herself contemplating mortality and crowd theory simultaneously.

That’s when she realized: she wasn’t late. Everyone was. And for one transcendent second, she achieved *collective equilibrium.*

IV. The Behavioral Dynamics

Public transport magnifies every cognitive bias known to man:

- **The Planning Fallacy:** “It’ll take 20 minutes today.” It never has.
- **Social Proof Bias:** “If they’re boarding, I must too.” The herd knows nothing.
- **Illusion of Fairness:** “I was here first.” Time disagrees.
- **Learned Helplessness:** The bus isn’t late. The universe is.

Each ride becomes a moral laboratory: how much inefficiency can civilization endure before collapsing into primal etiquette?

As it turns out — quite a lot. Humans may hate delays, but they love narratives of endurance.

V. Archetypes in the Transit Ecosystem

Archetype	Core Strategy	Distinguishing Behavior
The Doorway Philosopher	Guards the exit, blocks flow	Believes movement is conceptual

Archetype	Core Strategy	Distinguishing Behavior
The Seat Strategist	Calculates proximity to window & exit	Mistimes every stop
The Stoic Scroller	Retreats into phone	Achieves enlightenment by ignoring elbows
The Conversational Martyr	Complains audibly for communal bonding	Raises morale by lowering everyone's hope
The Driver-Guru	Controls chaos through horn and resignation	Understands systems theory viscerally

🗨 *Margin note:* "Every bus has its own corporate culture. You know it by how people queue — or don't."

VI. The Strategic Takeaway: Buffers, Bottlenecks, and Patience Elasticity

A **system** is only as resilient as its slack — the tiny margin between normal and catastrophe. Modern life, like public transport, runs with no slack. We optimize for efficiency until there's no room left for recovery.

In systems terms:

Resilience = Buffer ÷ Bottleneck Severity

The trick, therefore, is not speed, but **buffer design** — emotional and spatial. Leave earlier. Expect delay. Cultivate patience like a renewable resource.

Because while the city optimizes for throughput, you must optimize for sanity.

VII. Anecdote Two: The Bus Driver's Wisdom

One driver, when asked about delays, said quietly:

"I don't drive the bus. I drive time."

He wasn't being poetic; he was managing flow. He'd learned to brake not by speed but by crowd mood — faster when spirits high, slower when tension rose.

Systems thinkers call this **adaptive pacing.** Poets call it survival. Commuters call it "finally, someone who gets it."

VIII. The Corporate Parallel

Corporations resemble transport networks: endless queues, overloaded pipelines, bottlenecks masquerading as "process."

- The **email inbox** is a bus stop.
- The **manager** is the conductor who says, "Just one more passenger."
- The **meeting room** is the bottleneck where flow goes to die.

Every reorg promises "smoother throughput." Every quarter ends with a jam. What keeps the company (and the city) functioning is not perfect design — it's **collective tolerance for inefficiency.**

The unspoken contract:

"We will endure this together, because there's nowhere else to go."

IX. The Existential Undercurrent

Public transport is democracy at its most intimate. No hierarchy, no exclusivity, no VIP lane. Just people, pressed together, breathing the same shared impatience.

It's humbling. It's terrible. It's also civilization.

Every push, pause, and sigh is proof that the system, however flawed, still holds. Because the alternative — everyone driving alone — isn't freedom. It's entropy with parking fees.

X. The Moral (Standing Room Only)

Public transport teaches the grand paradox of systems: perfection breaks, imperfection bends.

Moral: A good system isn't one without friction — it's one that forgives it.

> **"Urban Flow Resilience Index (2025)"**
>
> *Institute for Everyday Systems Findings:* – Average bus operates at 138% capacity during peak hours. – 62% of commuters claim "patience development" as their primary soft skill. – 17% meditate without knowing it. Economists define public transport as **a slow-moving empathy simulator disguised as logistics.**

Epilogue Fragment: The Terminal Station

At last, the bus empties. You step out, disheveled yet calm, part of a vast system that somehow didn't collapse today. You glance back — the bus lurches forward, taking a new batch of optimists.

For a moment, you feel grateful for the chaos. It's the only system that still includes you.

CHAPTER XI

PARKING LOT DIPLOMACY

> *Or: Negotiation, brinkmanship, and the tragedy of the commons.*

I. The Situation

It's late. You're circling the office parking lot — an asphalt labyrinth of hope and hostility. You spot a car reversing out. Salvation!

But wait — another driver spots it too. Two vehicles approach the same rectangle of asphalt destiny.

Both slow down. Both flick indicators. You make eye contact — the human equivalent of a **geopolitical summit.**

In that moment, the world collapses into two possible futures:

- **You park.**
- **You become the anecdote.**

And thus begins the delicate art of **Parking Lot Diplomacy.**

II. The Model: The Game of Shared Scarcity

Parking, as a system, obeys the grim logic of the **Tragedy of the Commons** — when individual rationality leads to collective misery.

Each driver maximizes personal convenience ("closer to entrance = better"), but collectively we produce gridlock, honking, and moral decay.

Player Strategy	Immediate Gain	Long-Term Cost
Aggressively Pursue Closest Spot	Save 30 seconds	Earn 3 enemies
Circle Patiently	Gain inner peace	Lose 15 minutes of life
Block and Wait	Secure territory	Trigger local anarchy
Park Far and Walk	Lose 3 minutes	Gain moral superiority
Pretend to Leave (Fake Reverse)	Chaos	Instant karmic punishment

Economists model this as a **non-cooperative game**, but psychologists recognize it as a **collective identity crisis.**

III. Anecdotal Case Study: The Reverse-Standoff

Meet *Anil* and *Farah*, both eying the same spot at the mall. Anil edges forward, Farah reverses in at a 17° angle — a classic **mirror standoff.**

The tension builds. Other cars queue. Horns escalate. A bystander records it for social media — the new court of public arbitration.

Finally, Anil concedes, muttering about "the decay of civility." Farah exits her car, triumphant yet strangely guilty. She later describes the experience as "winning something not worth winning."

In that, she captures the essence of all modern negotiation.

IV. The Behavioral Dynamics

Parking isn't a logistics issue. It's **a crisis of self-importance.**

We treat spots as moral rewards — proof that the universe recognizes our effort. That's why losing one feels personal.

Cognitive forces at play:

- **Entitlement Bias:** "I've been driving longer; I deserve it."
- **Endowment Effect:** Once you've eyed a spot, it's emotionally yours.
- **Optimism Bias:** "Something closer will open up." (It won't.)
- **Confirmation Bias:** "I always find one here." (Statistically false.)

Hence, parking lots become mirrors — not of cars, but of character.

V. Archetypes in the Asphalt Ecosystem

Archetype	Core Strategy	Observable Behavior
The Alpha Parker	Claims spot through intimidation	Signals dominance via horn
The Diplomat	Waves others ahead	Regrets it instantly
The Gambler	Keeps circling for "something better"	Ends 300 metres away
The Zen Minimalist	Parks far and calls it fitness	Smiles while sweating
The Opportunist	Waits behind someone leaving	Blocks entire lane proudly

🗨 *Margin note:* "In every parking lot, there exists one car that's been stationary for days — a symbol of pure strategic inertia."

VI. The Strategic Takeaway: Brinkmanship and Bounded Rationality

The **Parking Game** illustrates the economics of brinkmanship — each player pushing the boundary of reason, hoping the other blinks first.

Like global powers, both sides escalate signals: – A subtle inch forward (*credible threat*). – Headlight flash (*tactical warning*). – Engine rev (*preparation for conflict*).

Yet, rationally, both lose — time, fuel, and dignity.

The key insight from systems thinking:

Efficiency declines as ego approaches 100% utilization.

In organizational terms, that's your quarterly meeting in motion.

VII. Anecdote Two: The Cooperative Equilibrium

During monsoon season, *Ravi* and *Sonal* reached the same spot simultaneously. Instead of competing, they smiled awkwardly and **split the spot diagonally** — half on the line, half on principle.

Passersby stared in disbelief. It was ugly, inefficient, and completely human. Both left with soaked shoes but dry consciences.

Economists would call it *suboptimal equilibrium.* Sociologists would call it *grace.*

VIII. The Corporate Parallel

Corporate life is a perpetual parking lot: too many vehicles (ambitions), too few spots (opportunities).

- Projects compete for visibility.
- Teams block each other while "waiting for approval."
- Executives reverse into spaces already taken by someone's "strategic initiative."

Every memo about "collaboration" is just a polite horn honk.

And the truly wise professionals? They park quietly, far from the spotlight — and reach the elevator first.

IX. The Existential Undercurrent

Parking lots are miniature utopias of controlled chaos. They expose the paradox of civilization: we build vast systems to save time, then spend that time fighting over rectangles.

The act of parking is our daily surrender to spatial limits — a ritual reminder that not every victory fits neatly within painted lines.

At its core, parking isn't about cars. It's about learning when to stop searching and simply **occupy what's available.**

X. The Moral (Still Circling)

The secret to happiness is not finding the perfect spot — it's accepting the imperfect one early.

Moral: Strategy isn't domination; it's graceful concession before you block the exit.

"Urban Parking Efficiency Index 2025"

Institute for Urban Patience (IUP) reports: – 73% of drivers claim "someone stole their spot." – 48% admit doing the same. – 5% say they "believe in karma," usually while parking illegally. Economists define parking as **an emotional market with infinite demand and finite humility.**

Epilogue Fragment: The Long Walk

You park far away. As you walk toward your destination, you spot another car taking "your" spot. You smile. You feel — unexpectedly — free.

The distance, it turns out, is the price of serenity. And for once, it feels like a bargain.

CHAPTER XII

THE GROCERY BASKET PARADOX

> *Or: Scope creep, marginal utility, and the discount-induced distortion.*

I. The Situation

It begins, as all fiscal tragedies do, with a simple intention. You walk into the supermarket with a list so modest it could fit on a Post-it: *milk, bread, detergent.*

Fifty-three minutes later, you emerge pushing a trolley that looks like it belongs to a mid-sized family of raccoons. You whisper something defensive like, *"They were on offer."*

Congratulations — you've just completed a live demonstration of **scope creep** in a low-stakes project environment.

II. The Model: From Shopping List to Project Failure

Economists talk of **marginal utility** — the extra satisfaction gained from consuming one more unit of something. In supermarkets, this function is concave — each extra snack yields less joy, but more regret.

Concept	Supermarket Equivalent	Corporate Analogue
Planned Scope	3 essential items	Original project charter

Concept	Supermarket Equivalent	Corporate Analogue
Scope Creep	+ 12 "just in case" add-ons	Feature inflation
Change Request	"Let's try that new brand."	Executive whim
Budget Variance	+ ₹ 780 at checkout	Fiscal quarter shock
Post-Implementation Review	Fridge audit at home	After-action blame cycle

Every unplanned item represents a moment of **bounded rationality** — you were making the best possible decision with limited willpower and aggressive lighting.

III. Anecdotal Case Study: The Discount Distortion

Meet *Rohit*, a rational man until he enters a store with the words "Buy One Get One Free." He buys two family-sized ketchups though he lives alone. He calculates he's "saved ₹ 120," then spends ₹ 400 on chips to "justify the saving."

Behavioral economists call this the **discount induced distortion** — where the brain confuses spending with saving so completely that wallets become performative.

By the time Rohit reaches checkout, he has secured the moral equivalent of a corporate cost-saving initiative that doubles expenses.

IV. The Behavioral Dynamics

Supermarkets are architecture in the service of impulse. They weaponize psychology with the precision of a management consultant.

Biases in play:

- **Anchoring Effect:** The first price you see frames what feels cheap.
- **Decoy Effect:** A large size exists only to make the medium look reasonable.
- **Endowment Effect:** Once you touch it, you own it emotionally.
- **Sunk Cost Fallacy:** "I've come this far down the aisle…"

It's not a store. It's a simulation of free will with checkout lanes.

V. Archetypes of the Aisle

Archetype	Core Strategy	Typical Outcome
The List Follower	Adheres to plan heroically	Falls at the snack aisle
The Explorer	Browses for "inspiration"	Discovers existential emptiness
The Bulk Economist	Buys family packs for one	Owns rice till 2042
The Brand-Switcher	Seeks novelty	Complains about change
The Coupon Hoarder	Optimizes to death	Delays checkout for everyone

🗨 *Margin note:* "Every cart contains the story of a person who once believed they had self-control."

VI. The Strategic Takeaway: Scope Control and Decision Fatigue

In project management terms, the Grocery Basket Paradox demonstrates two key truths:

1. **Scope Creep is Inevitable.** Humans cannot resist adding "small extras." The only control mechanism is checkout panic.
2. **Marginal Utility Declines Faster Than Self-Justification.** After the fifth "treat," pleasure plateaus but rationalization soars.

Strategic translation: learn to quit while you still feel under-rewarded. Satisfaction peaks not when the basket is full, but when discipline barely holds.

VII. Anecdote Two: The Household Budget Summit

When *Meera and Rajat* sat down for their monthly expense review, they found grocery spending up 30%. Rajat blamed inflation. Meera blamed Rajat's hunger during shopping. They implemented a "two-list policy": one essential, one "exploratory."

Within weeks, the exploratory list had tripled in size. Meera declared a temporary moratorium on new brands. Rajat called it "an agile response to market conditions."

Their relationship survived, but the pantry remains a museum of impulse.

VIII. The Corporate Parallel

Every organization runs a metaphorical supermarket: the roadmap. Teams start with a clear list of objectives. Then someone adds "low-hanging fruit." Then someone else adds "stretch goals." Before long, you're paying for features no one uses and celebrating "cross-functional alignment."

Quarter ends. Budgets bloat. Executives declare "strategic synergies." In truth, they've just bought two family-sized ketchups of their own.

IX. The Existential Undercurrent

Shopping isn't about need; it's about control — a small, structured arena where you can feel decisive. Each choice is a tiny affirmation that you still know what you want. Until, of course, you realize you don't.

Maybe the aisle isn't a marketplace but a mirror. And every cart rolling toward checkout is just another person trying to fill a metaphorical deficit with literal snacks.

X. The Moral (At Checkout)

Efficiency is not in buying what's cheap, but in leaving what's unnecessary.

Moral: True strategy is not optimizing the basket — it's knowing when to push it away.

> **"Household Cart Analytics 2025"**
>
> *Institute for Domestic Decision Science reports:* – 81 % of shoppers overspend by 25 % per trip. – 42 % claim they "stick to the list." Only 12 % actually do. – 100 % believe they'll "do better next time." Economists classify the supermarket as **a controlled experiment in rational failure.**

Epilogue Fragment: The Fridge Audit

You unpack at home, marvel at your purchases, and feel briefly in control. A week later, half the vegetables have expired, and you're ordering take-out.

You stare at the fridge, half empty and half aspirational, and think:

"I should make a list next time." You will. It won't matter.

ARC III: THE SOCIAL SUPPLY CHAIN

FRIENDS, FAVORS, AND SOCIAL CAPITAL

CHAPTER XIII

THE WHATSAPP GROUP AS A MINI-ECOSYSTEM

> *Or: Coordination cost, information overload, and the signaling economy.*

I. The Situation

There was a time when "staying in touch" meant effort. Now, it means *being trapped in a chatroom you can never ethically leave.*

You open WhatsApp. The unread count mocks you — *132 messages* in a group named "College Legends 🔥🔥🔥." The last thing you remember, they were planning a reunion. The conversation has since evolved into a three-day debate about mutual funds, cricket, and someone's toddler's drawing of a dragon.

You scroll, you sigh, you mute — the modern equivalent of meditation. And as the blue ticks march on, you realize: this is not communication. This is **crowdsourced entropy.**

II. The Model: Coordination Cost and Network Complexity

Economists studying organizational behavior once spoke of **transaction costs** — the hidden frictions of coordinating effort. WhatsApp groups are their natural experiment in ungoverned coordination.

In theory, every member increases potential connection value. In reality, each new addition doubles confusion.

Group Size (n)	Possible Communication Links = n(n–1)/2	Resulting State
3	3	Manageable chaos
5	10	Consensus impossible
12	66	Meme economy forms
20+	190+	Civilization collapses

Welcome to **Metcalfe's Law of Madness:**

The value of a WhatsApp group increases with the square of its members — until it becomes infinite and therefore useless.

III. Anecdotal Case Study: The Reunion That Never Was

Consider *Batch 2006*, a once-proud group now operating as a digital commune. Initial purpose: organize reunion. Outcome: 734 messages, 0 reunions, 12 side arguments about restaurant choices, and one brief schism over "political neutrality."

By month two, sub-groups had formed — "2006 Core," "2006 Delhi," "2006 Re-Reunion," and "No Politics Please." Eventually, someone suggested creating a Google Sheet. No one filled it.

Sociologists would call this **emergent complexity.** The participants call it *bonding.*

IV. The Behavioral Dynamics

Human attention is a scarce resource — yet we treat it as if Costco sells it in bulk.

The WhatsApp group exploits several key behavioral weaknesses:

- **Social Proof Bias:** We respond to prove we're "still part of the tribe."
- **Signaling Theory:** Every sticker, emoji, or "😂" is a micro-expression of loyalty.
- **Information Cascades:** Once one person sends "Good morning 🌞," twelve follow.
- **Reciprocity Pressure:** If someone sends birthday wishes, you *must* reply — even if the original wish was algorithmically remembered.

Thus, the group sustains itself not by relevance but by inertia.

V. Archetypes in the Group Ecosystem

Archetype	Core Strategy	Observable Behavior
The Alpha Texter	Posts first and most	Believes silence = dissent
The Lurker	Reads everything, says nothing	Silent custodian of gossip
The Meme Distributor	Propagates cultural inflation	Mistakes quantity for wit
The Archivist	Forwards old photos weekly	Nostalgia as leadership
The Flamer	Occasionally stirs conflict	Keeps engagement metrics high

🗨 *Margin note:* "If engagement is the new currency, your cousin's daily 'Good Morning' GIF is the Federal Reserve."

VI. The Strategic Takeaway: The Economy of Signaling

Each message in a WhatsApp group is a **signal** — an attempt to assert identity, alliance, or relevance. But when everyone signals simultaneously, the signal-to-noise ratio collapses.

In systems terms:

Meaning Density (MD) = Total Messages ÷ Genuine Insights.

Across most groups, MD approaches zero by Day 3. And yet, the network persists — because belonging is more valuable than clarity.

The strategic lesson? When coordination cost exceeds informational value, **ritual replaces purpose.** In WhatsApp, as in organizations, the meeting continues long after the agenda is forgotten.

VII. Anecdote Two: The Exit Strategy

When *Ritika* finally decided to leave "The Family Chat (Official)," she rehearsed her message for two hours. She typed: "Going off WhatsApp for a bit, love you all ♡ ." Then hesitated. What if they took it personally?

She muted the group for one year instead — a **soft exit** now standard in diplomacy and marriage. The group, unaware, continues tagging her in festival greetings. She remains simultaneously gone and present — a Schrödinger's participant.

VIII. The Corporate Parallel

A WhatsApp group is a miniature organization without leadership, agenda, or HR—which is to say, most organizations.

- Every "Good morning" is a corporate memo in disguise.
- Every "LOL" is performative alignment.
- Every unread message count is the cost of not setting boundaries.

Slack channels, Teams groups, and email threads differ only in tone and fonts. The lesson scales perfectly: **Communication multiplies faster than understanding.**

IX. The Existential Undercurrent

The group's real function is comfort through noise — proof that the world still knows your name, even if it spells it wrong in memes.

These chatrooms are our digital campfires: they provide warmth, flicker unpredictably, and occasionally burn the house down. They turn nostalgia into infrastructure. And though we complain, we never truly leave — because being "in the loop" feels safer than being at peace.

X. The Moral (Muted for One Year)

Participation is overrated. Presence is enough.

Moral: The wisest member of every group is the one who reads everything, replies to nothing, and still gets tagged in every birthday post.

"Network Attention Index (2025)"

Institute for Applied Social Capital Studies reports: – Average adult is in 18.6 WhatsApp groups. – 76 % mute at least half of them. – 92 % still feel guilty about not responding. Sociologists classify WhatsApp as **a high-latency coordination tool powered by FOMO and obligation.**

Epilogue Fragment: The Archive of Echoes

At 2 a.m., your phone buzzes — someone revived a long-dead thread with "Anyone remember this trip?" You open it. Old photos. Familiar names. Laughter bubbles faintly.

For a moment, it feels like coming home. Then another message: *"Add me to the new group?"* And you realize — ecosystems don't end. They just migrate.

CHAPTER XIV

FRIENDSHIP ROI

> *Or: Portfolio theory applied to emotional investments.*

I. The Situation

At some point in adulthood, you realize friendship operates like an underperforming stock portfolio: high on nostalgia, low on liquidity, and occasionally prone to delisting.

You think of your friends not as people you see, but as names you *should* text more often. You scroll through your contact list like a guilt-ridden fund manager reviewing dormant assets.

Some have appreciated (they still reply with warmth). Some have depreciated (they now "seen" your messages without context). And some have merged into entirely new entities — *"family friends."*

Friendship, you conclude, is not a feeling. It's an unregulated market.

II. The Model: Portfolio Theory of Emotional Capital

Finance tells us that risk and return are inseparable — the higher the emotional investment, the greater the volatility.

Friendship Type	Expected Return	Emotional Volatility	Liquidity
Childhood Bond	Warm, stable nostalgia	Low	High (annual call on birthdays)
Work Ally	Tactical utility, moral support	Medium	Variable (changes with org chart)
Party Acquaintance	Short-term excitement	High	None
Confidant	Deep emotional ROI	Extremely volatile	Requires regular maintenance
Social Media Mutual	Inflated perceived value	Synthetic volatility	Entirely illiquid

Modern adulthood, therefore, is about portfolio rebalancing — allocating time between *legacy assets* (old friends), *growth equities* (new connections), and *toxic derivatives* (people you're still friends with for sentimental reasons).

III. Anecdotal Case Study: The Diversification Fallacy

Ananya, age 32, once declared she would "keep in touch with everyone." She maintained separate WhatsApp lists — "School," "College," "Work," "Book Club," "Yoga Gang."

After a year, she'd developed chronic social fatigue and 138 unread birthday reminders. Her social capital had become a **diversified fatigue portfolio** — widespread exposure, zero intimacy.

She now focuses on three people and claims a 400% increase in "emotional yield." Economists call this *strategic concentration.* Therapists call it *boundaries.*

IV. The Behavioral Dynamics

Friendship is riddled with irrational investor behavior:

- **Loss Aversion:** We avoid ending stagnant friendships, fearing guilt more than wasted time.
- **Overconfidence Bias:** We assume we're "good at keeping in touch." Evidence disagrees.
- **Sunk Cost Fallacy:** "We've been friends so long…" is emotional deadweight phrased romantically.
- **Recency Bias:** We overvalue whoever we spoke to last, regardless of depth.

Thus, friendship management becomes less about love and more about maintenance — the quiet art of preventing social inflation.

V. Archetypes in the Emotional Market

Archetype	Core Strategy	Observable Behavior
The High-Frequency Texter	Trades affection daily	Suffers chronic burnout
The Long-Term Holder	Keeps small circle	Gains steady dividends
The Nostalgic Investor	Obsesses over past friendships	Hoards emotional junk bonds
The Opportunistic Connector	Networks aggressively	Mistakes volume for value

Archetype	Core Strategy	Observable Behavior
The Ghost	Withdraws silently	Maintains mystique, no returns

🗨 *Margin note:* "Every friend is a stock. Some split. Some crash. Some quietly pay dividends in memes."

VI. The Strategic Takeaway: Diversify, but Not to Death

Portfolio theory teaches us that diversification reduces risk but also dilutes focus. The same applies to friendship — too many "weak ties" leave little room for genuine bandwidth.

In social capital terms:

Net Emotional Return (NER) = Meaning ÷ Maintenance Cost

When maintenance exceeds meaning, divest. That doesn't make you cold; it makes you solvent.

Friendship, like any portfolio, thrives on rebalancing — not ruthless exits, but honest audits.

VII. Anecdote Two: The Quarterly Review

Every December, *Vikram* conducts his "Friendship Audit." He scrolls through his chat list, marking people he hasn't spoken to in 12 months. For each, he sends a message: *"Hey, how have you been?"*

Replies fall into three categories:

- "Hey! So good to hear from you." (mutual guilt dividend)
- "Who's this?" (asset write-off)
- Seen–no reply (permanent impairment).

Vikram's ROI is modest but steady. His friendships are fewer, his heart lighter, and his notifications fewer. He calls it *emotional decluttering.*

VIII. The Corporate Parallel

Corporations, too, mismanage relationships. They hoard contacts, chase "strategic partnerships," and brag about "strong networks." Yet, their real value lies in *trusted collaborations,* not volume.

In business as in friendship, the most stable networks rely on **trust liquidity** — the ability to mobilize goodwill quickly. When that's gone, all that remains is a list of contacts with expired credit.

IX. The Existential Undercurrent

Friendship, at its core, is irrational. You invest not for returns but for the rare pleasure of being understood without footnotes. It's a market that defies equilibrium — volatile, cyclical, and occasionally miraculous.

And maybe that's the point: love isn't efficient, it's generous. You don't diversify friendship to minimize loss; you diversify to spread joy's risk.

Because the only real bankruptcies are the ones where you stop trying.

X. The Moral (Unread Message Pending)

You can't optimize connection. You can only cherish volatility.

Moral: Friendship isn't about managing risk — it's about occasionally accepting emotional drawdown for the joy of compound laughter.

> **"Social Capital Index 2025"**
>
> *Institute for Interpersonal Economics reports:* – Average adult maintains 6 "active" friendships. – 72 % say they "should reach out more." – 51 % keep at least one zombie chat alive. Sociologists classify friendship as **a high-risk, low-efficiency asset class with priceless intrinsic value.**

Epilogue Fragment: The Silent Dividend

One evening, an old friend texts out of nowhere: *"Hey, remember that terrible road trip?"* You laugh aloud. The memory surfaces intact, bright, absurd.

No ROI calculation needed. Some assets just keep compounding quietly in the background — interest paid in laughter.

CHAPTER XV

THE FAVOR BANK

Or: Reciprocity and liquidity crises in social lending.

I. The Situation

You lend a friend your Netflix password. They borrow your car "just for the weekend." You help a colleague move house, and three years later you're still waiting for your karma dividend.

Friendships, it turns out, are not sustained by love alone — they're lubricated by a steady flow of *informal obligations.* Every "Can you just help me with…" is a microloan in the shadow economy of goodwill.

And like all financial systems, the Favor Bank runs on **trust, selective memory, and mild resentment.**

II. The Model: Social Liquidity and the Law of Reciprocity

The Favor Bank operates much like a decentralized credit market — unregulated, emotionally volatile, and prone to collapses during wedding seasons.

Principle	Financial Analogue	Social Equivalent
Creditworthiness	Repayment reliability	"He actually returns calls."

Principle	Financial Analogue	Social Equivalent
Interest Rate	Emotional effort required	"She owes me *big time.*"
Liquidity	Availability to help	"I'd love to, but…"
Default Risk	Unreciprocated favor	"He never even said thanks."
Market Shock	Crisis of guilt or pride	"I didn't *ask* for help!"

Reciprocity — the backbone of human cooperation — is essentially **emotional accounting**. We help because we expect future returns, however vaguely defined.

The trick, of course, is pretending we don't.

III. Anecdotal Case Study: The Moving-Day Default

When *Ravi* helped his friend *Karan* move apartments, he told himself, "That's what friends are for." Two months later, Ravi's own move came up — Karan was "busy that weekend."

Ravi smiled it off, but internally restructured Karan's rating from "Prime Borrower" to "High Risk." He stopped sharing memes with him for six weeks — a soft sanction in the emotional markets.

Thus was born the first liquidity crisis in their friendship.

IV. The Behavioral Dynamics

The Favor Bank's psychology rests on four ancient fallacies:

1. **Symmetry Assumption:** We expect others to value favors as much as we do.
2. **Recency Effect:** The last favor defines the current balance.
3. **Illusion of Altruism:** We tell ourselves we're helping selflessly — until we're not.
4. **Selective Accounting:** We remember every favor we gave, but only 40% of those received.

In behavioral finance terms, the Favor Bank is a perfect storm of **asymmetric perception and moral inflation.**

V. Archetypes in the Favor Economy

Archetype	Core Strategy	Observable Behavior
The Banker	Keeps detailed mental ledger	Often says, "After all I've done for you…"
The Philanthropist	Helps unconditionally	Secretly tracks spiritual ROI
The Opportunist	Asks for everything, offers nothing	Defaults cheerfully
The Transactionalist	Balances instantly	"You helped me move, I brought you pizza — we're square."
The Silent Defaulter	Ghosts after receiving help	Returns three years later like an emerging market

🗨 *Margin note:* "A favor unpaid is never forgotten — just quietly compounded."

VI. The Strategic Takeaway: Reciprocity as Currency

Social capital functions on **perceived fairness**, not perfect bookkeeping. In systems terms, equilibrium is emotional, not numerical.

The system fails when favors feel like debt instead of dignity.

Healthy networks maintain **liquidity** — favors flow freely, replenished by gratitude, not guilt. Tight, mistrustful networks hoard help — everyone waits for others to move first.

That's not friendship; that's a liquidity trap.

VII. Anecdote Two: The Festival Bailout

During Diwali, *Anita* forgot to bring sweets to the office potluck. Her colleague *Priya* shared hers, saying, "It's fine, next time." Next time never came.

A year later, Anita helped Priya meet a client deadline by editing her presentation slides at midnight. Neither mentioned the sweets. Both felt quietly even.

That's how mature economies work — not through repayment, but through equilibrium drift.

VIII. The Corporate Parallel

Organizations, too, run on favor banks. Every time you "just help" a coworker with a deck, or "cover" for someone in a meeting, you're trading in social currency.

Smart leaders cultivate **trust liquidity** — they give before they need. Weak cultures, on the other hand, run on IOUs — "I'll remember this" becomes the corporate version of emotional debt collection.

The difference between collaboration and exploitation? Whether your help feels like investment or taxation.

IX. The Existential Undercurrent

The Favor Bank is proof that humanity's oldest currency isn't gold or credit — it's gratitude. It's fragile, invisible, and yet the only asset that appreciates when given away.

Maybe the trick is to stop treating every kind act as a future claim. To offer, not to obligate. To receive, not to owe. To let the market of kindness float freely.

Because once you start keeping score, you've already gone bankrupt.

X. The Moral (Interest Accrued)

Kindness is valuable precisely because it's inefficient.

Moral: In the long run, generosity beats interest — and friendship remains solvent through periodic write-offs.

"Social Liquidity Index 2025"

Institute for Behavioral Reciprocity reports: – 68 % of adults admit they "keep informal favor tallies." – 44 % experience "repayment anxiety." – 12 % openly declare "emotional bankruptcy." Economists define the Favor Bank as **a self-regulating emotional economy with no central bank — only mutual delusion.**

Epilogue Fragment: The Ledger at Rest

Late at night, you think of someone you haven't spoken to in a while — someone who once helped you move, or listened without agenda. You smile. You message them, not to repay, but to thank.

No transaction. No balance sheet. Just the quiet satisfaction of settling the only debt that matters: remembrance.

CHAPTER XVI

FOMO AND COMPETITIVE BENCHMARKING

> *Or: How envy became the new KPI.*

I. The Situation

You wake up. Before your brain can even load its personality, your thumb opens Instagram.

Your friend from college has just finished a marathon. Another is in Bali "finding herself" (for the third time). Someone else is posing with a new car, captioned "#gratitude."

You, meanwhile, are still trying to find matching socks.

You tell yourself it doesn't bother you — that you're "happy for them." And yet, as you sip your reheated coffee, you feel the faint sting of invisible competition.

Congratulations — you've entered the **Global Leaderboard of Emotional Economics.**

II. The Model: Social Benchmarking and the Illusion of Progress

Classical economics assumes people seek to maximize *utility*. Modern psychology knows better: people seek to maximize *relative satisfaction*.

In other words — it's not what you have, it's how it stacks up on the feed.

Variable	Traditional Metric	FOMO Metric
Wealth	Actual income	How expensive your vacation looks
Fitness	Health	Number of fitness selfies
Happiness	Inner peace	Sunset photo frequency
Career Success	Job satisfaction	LinkedIn announcement volume
Relationship Quality	Mutual respect	Couple trip photogenicity

You are no longer competing for resources; you're competing for *relevance.*

III. Anecdotal Case Study: The Birthday Party Benchmark

Rhea threw a small dinner for her birthday — eight friends, laughter, dim lighting, sincere joy. The next day, she opened Instagram.

Her colleague *Tanya* had hosted a "birthday weekend" in Goa, complete with drone footage, branded cupcakes, and a hashtag: **#TanyaTurns30InStyle.**

By lunchtime, Rhea was Googling "Affordable drone rentals in Mumbai."

Behavioral economists call this *reference-dependent utility* — satisfaction that decays with every scroll.

IV. The Behavioral Dynamics

At its core, FOMO is a misfiring of the brain's ancient **social survival algorithm**. In hunter-gatherer days, missing out meant starvation. In 2025, it means being untagged.

Psychological biases driving the cycle:

- **Social Comparison Bias:** We evaluate ourselves through others' visible metrics.
- **Availability Heuristic:** We mistake visibility for frequency — everyone seems more active because they're more online.
- **Survivorship Bias:** We only see successes, never their failures.
- **Loss Aversion:** Missing out *hurts* more than participation *pleases.*

Thus, we scroll not to connect but to audit — an endless quarterly review of our own inadequacy.

V. Archetypes in the FOMO Economy

Archetype	Core Strategy	Observable Behavior
The Chronic Poster	Signals abundance	Secretly exhausted
The Benchmark Analyst	Tracks others' progress meticulously	Calls it "inspiration"
The Silent Scroller	Consumes envy quietly	Develops strong opinions on Bali resorts
The Humblebragger	Camouflages achievement as modesty	"Can't believe this happened 🗨"

Archetype	Core Strategy	Observable Behavior
The Digital Minimalist	Publicly rejects FOMO	Checks everyone's Stories at night

🗨 *Margin note:* "In the market of self-worth, envy is the inflation nobody admits to causing."

VI. The Strategic Takeaway: The KPI of Contentment

FOMO is not about missing events; it's about missing *validation.* Every scroll is a mini performance review — except the metrics are arbitrary and the boss is imaginary.

From a strategy lens:

Benchmarking without context creates motion without progress.

In corporate settings, companies that obsess over competitor metrics end up mirroring their mediocrity. Likewise, individuals chasing social parity end up optimizing for aesthetics over authenticity.

The antidote is *Internal Benchmarking* — comparing yourself not to others' highlight reels but to your own baselines.

Progress is personal. Relevance is rented.

VII. Anecdote Two: The Vacation Vortex

Arjun took a break from work to "recharge." He avoided social media for seven days — bliss, silence, sunrise. On day eight, he posted a beach photo.

It got 37 likes. His friend *Ravi,* meanwhile, posted a gym mirror selfie: 226 likes.

By sunset, Arjun had scheduled another vacation — this time "somewhere more Instagrammable."

Economists would call this a **feedback loop of envy elasticity.** Philosophers might just call it *sad.*

VIII. The Corporate Parallel

In business, benchmarking drives performance — until it drives obsession. Companies imitate competitors' KPIs, losing sight of their unique advantage. That's FOMO in a tie.

Every "industry best practice" started as someone else's panic-induced reaction. Likewise, every human chasing the next big thing is simply benchmarking someone else's illusion.

Strategic maturity — in both boardrooms and lives — comes from realizing that differentiation beats imitation.

IX. The Existential Undercurrent

The real cost of FOMO isn't money or time — it's presence. Every minute spent imagining a better elsewhere is one stolen from the imperfect, glorious *here.*

Envy, at its purest, is a yearning for coherence — the wish that your narrative made as much sense as others' captions. But the truth is: everyone's feed is a stitched-together PowerPoint of curated chaos. No one's life is as smooth as their filters.

The tragedy isn't missing out on others' moments; it's missing your own.

X. The Moral (Post Unavailable)

Comparison is the thief of joy — and the accountant of insecurity.

Moral: True strategy is not outpacing others; it's deleting the scoreboard entirely.

> **"The Envy Economy 2025"**
>
> *Institute for Competitive Happiness Studies reports:* – 71 % of users feel "mild discontent" after scrolling social media. – 49 % admit to "posting for validation." – 8 % claim to be "above it all." None of them are. Behavioral economists define FOMO as **a self-reinforcing market bubble in perceived happiness.**

Epilogue Fragment: The Quiet Benchmark

You silence notifications for a week. You still live, laugh, and eat noodles in peace. Nothing collapses. The world spins without your metrics.

And in that quiet, you realize — perhaps the highest KPI of all is **indifference.**

CHAPTER XVII

THE NETWORKING FALLACY

> *Or: Efficiency vs. authenticity in relationship-building.*

I. The Situation

You walk into a networking event. You've ironed your shirt, rehearsed your "elevator pitch," and promised yourself you'll "put yourself out there."

Thirty minutes in, you've shaken fourteen hands, forgotten twelve names, and are now standing near the snacks table pretending to check your phone. You feel like a corporate Pokémon — exchanging business cards instead of abilities.

And yet, everyone insists this is "how connections are made."

What they don't tell you is: you're in an economy where **attention is currency and authenticity is inflationary.**

II. The Model: The Relationship Efficiency Curve

Networking, at least in theory, is a *returns-to-scale problem.*

Phase	Investment (Effort)	Expected ROI (Authentic Connection)	Actual Outcome
0–5 contacts	Moderate	High	Real rapport possible
5–20 contacts	High	Medium	Memory begins to blur

Phase	Investment (Effort)	Expected ROI (Authentic Connection)	Actual Outcome
20–50 contacts	Exhausting	Low	"We should catch up sometime!"
50+ contacts	Unsustainable	Zero	Relationship fatigue sets in

This follows a classic **diminishing returns** curve — authenticity peaks early and erodes under efficiency pressure. What begins as conversation becomes *CRM management.*

III. Anecdotal Case Study: The Conference Conversion Rate

At an industry summit, *Raghav* collected 72 business cards in one evening. He proudly uploaded them to his "networking tracker" spreadsheet.

Three months later, only two of those people remembered him. One had confused him with another "Raghav." The other wanted to sell him SaaS software.

Raghav updated his spreadsheet's final column to read: "Outcome — existential reflection."

Economists might call this a **negative ROI on social capital.** Philosophers would just call it *being human.*

IV. The Behavioral Dynamics

Why do we over-network? Because the corporate world gamifies relationships.

Key biases at play:

- **Quantity Illusion:** More connections = more opportunity. (False.)
- **Reciprocity Bias:** "They'll help me someday." (They won't.)
- **Survivorship Bias:** We only hear success stories — "I met my co-founder at a conference!" — never the other 999 awkward handshakes.
- **Optimism Bias:** "This time, I'll follow up." (You won't.)

Networking thus becomes a ritual of *social insurance*, not genuine curiosity — a hedge against future obscurity.

V. Archetypes at the Mixer

Archetype	Core Strategy	Observable Behavior
The Card Collector	Maximizes volume	Treats conversation as KPI
The Elevator Pitcher	Delivers pre-scripted monologue	Exhales only when done
The Shadow Networker	Hovers silently on LinkedIn	Likes posts at 2 a.m.
The Empathic Outlier	Asks genuine questions	Leaves early, soul intact
The Thought Leader	Says "synergy" unironically	Monologues disguised as dialogue

🗨 *Margin note:* "Networking events are like speed dating for people who hate both speed and dating."

VI. The Strategic Takeaway: Efficiency Kills Empathy

Networking's great illusion is that relationships can be optimized. But empathy doesn't scale — it *simmers.*

In economic terms, **authenticity is a non-scalable asset.** You can't mass-produce it without devaluing it.

True connections emerge from *shared vulnerability*, not *shared LinkedIn hashtags.* The moment you start thinking in conversion rates, you've already outsourced sincerity to your CRM.

The wiser strategy? Fewer meetings, deeper meanings.

VII. Anecdote Two: The Barista Bond

After years of forced conferences, *Nisha* realized her most valuable "network" wasn't her industry peers — it was the barista at the café she frequented daily.

He remembered her deadlines, her preferred roast, and once even caught her typo on a presentation printout. She got more support — and perspective — from him than from any professional "connection."

Sociologists would call that **informal social capital.** She calls it *Tuesday.*

VIII. The Corporate Parallel

Organizations suffer the same fallacy. They obsess over *stakeholder mapping*, *relationship management systems*, and *"network leverage."* Yet, their real breakthroughs often come from unplanned hallway conversations — the human equivalent of a coffee spill leading to innovation.

The moral for companies and individuals alike:

Culture beats contact lists. Trust beats traction.

Because while networking builds reach, only sincerity builds resilience.

IX. The Existential Undercurrent

We mistake proximity for intimacy. We confuse being *known* with being *understood.*

Networking promises belonging, but delivers busyness — a blur of names without narratives. It flatters our egos while starving our souls.

Perhaps the real question isn't "Who do I know?" but "Who do I still like being silent with?"

X. The Moral (Connection Pending…)

Networking is about planting seeds, not collecting saplings.

Moral: Relationships, like gardens, don't grow faster when you water everything.

"The Authenticity Index 2025"

Institute for Human Capital Studies reports: – 82 % of professionals feel "networking fatigue." – 67 % admit to "forgetting names immediately." – 39 % maintain contacts "for optics." Economists define networking as **a low-yield social investment with occasional serendipitous windfalls.**

Epilogue Fragment: The Forgotten Contact

Weeks later, you find a business card in your jacket pocket. You don't remember the face — only the handshake.

You smile, toss it into the bin, and message an old friend instead. Connection restored. Network optimized — finally, for meaning.

CHAPTER XVIII

THE SOCIAL MEDIA STRATEGY SPIRAL

Or: Managing brand "You" in an attention economy.

I. The Situation

It starts innocently enough. You post a sunset photo. You write a caption that sounds humble but elegant — *"Grateful for small moments* ."

The likes trickle in. Dopamine pings. You smile. Then you post again. And again.

Soon, you're no longer living moments; you're producing them. Dinner is content. Books are props. Even your cat's existential stare is "relatable engagement."

You've become **Chief Marketing Officer of Yourself, Inc.** The problem? The audience never sleeps, and neither does your insecurity.

II. The Model: The Attention Economy Flywheel

In economics, growth loops fuel expansion. In social media, *validation loops* fuel self-delusion.

Stage	Input	Output	Side Effect
1. Content Creation	"Share a thought"	Visibility	Mild anxiety

Stage	Input	Output	Side Effect
2. Engagement Surge	Likes, comments, DMs	Dopamine	Addictive behavior
3. Optimization	Better lighting, tighter captions	Increased reach	Decreased sincerity
4. Feedback Fatigue	Algorithmic plateau	Despair	"Shadowban paranoia"
5. Pivot	Rebrand as "authentic"	Momentary relevance	Cycle restarts

Thus begins the **Social Media Strategy Spiral** — a self-reinforcing loop where meaning is monetized and identity becomes iterative.

III. Anecdotal Case Study: The Influencer's Dilemma

Ritika started a small food page "just for fun." A year later, she had 50,000 followers, three sponsorships, and constant performance anxiety. She found herself plating meals for photos she didn't actually eat.

One day, she realized she'd spent 40 minutes arranging avocado toast and 2 minutes consuming it. Her therapist called it *symbolic burnout.* Her followers called it *aesthetic consistency.*

Behavioral economists might call it **attention arbitrage gone wrong.**

IV. The Behavioral Dynamics

The platform economy exploits our **narcissism–insecurity feedback loop.** It sells validation as empowerment while extracting data as tribute.

Cognitive biases in play:

- **Availability Bias:** The more others post, the more you feel compelled to.
- **Social Proof Bias:** Engagement metrics replace genuine feedback.
- **Hedonic Adaptation:** Each milestone dulls faster than the last.
- **Performative Authenticity:** The curated illusion of uncurated life.

It's a system that converts *being seen* into a commodity — and then charges you for the exposure.

V. Archetypes in the Digital Agora

Archetype	Core Strategy	Observable Behavior
The Curator	Crafts immaculate feeds	Claims it's "just for fun"
The Philosopher	Posts profound quotes	Forgets to apply them
The Serial Rebrander	Changes bio quarterly	"Finding my niche ✨"
The Ghost Poster	Drops content, vanishes	Mysterious engagement spike
The Algorithm Agnostic	"I don't care about likes"	Checks stats every 12 minutes

Margin note: "Nothing says freedom like scheduling your authenticity for 9:30 a.m."

VI. The Strategic Takeaway: The Perils of Personal IPO

Social media is a perpetual IPO — *Initial Persona Offering.* You list fragments of yourself on the open market of attention, praying for steady valuation.

But as with any market, overexposure leads to volatility. The more you optimize for reach, the more you dilute for resonance.

In brand terms:

Differentiation thrives on depth, not display.

Real strategy isn't growing your audience — it's retaining your identity when the algorithm pivots.

VII. Anecdote Two: The Algorithmic Awakening

Kabir, a once-devoted content creator, went viral for a humorous post about office life. Overnight, 10,000 followers arrived. He tried to recreate the magic — daily posts, memes, captions — but engagement fell.

One night, he posted a plain text update:

"Honestly, I'm tired."

It got twice the likes of anything else. For a moment, he thought he'd found authenticity. Then he noticed people commenting: *"So raw 😍," "Love the vulnerability!"*

The spiral had merely rebranded itself.

VIII. The Corporate Parallel

Corporations do this too. They chase virality through "purpose campaigns," "humanizing their brand," or "joining conversations." But the more they try to appear human, the more algorithmic they become.

Employees mimic influencers, CEOs tweet like teenagers, and customer service adopts the tone of therapy.

The boardroom lesson?

You can't market sincerity; you must live it — or risk becoming a meme.

IX. The Existential Undercurrent

The tragedy of social media is that it amplifies our longing to matter — and then monetizes it. It promises connection but delivers performance anxiety. It offers a voice but demands constant speaking.

The philosopher might say: "We no longer express to connect; we express to exist." The strategist might add: "And we're being A/B tested for relatability."

Perhaps true liberation is to become gloriously unmarketable — to exist without hashtags, to eat without posting, to vanish without announcement.

X. The Moral (Engagement Rate: Irrelevant)

The best content isn't seen — it's lived.

Moral: In an attention economy, the rarest luxury is indifference.

> **"Influencer Economics 2025"**
>
> *Institute for Digital Selfhood reports:* – 74 % of adults curate their online persona. – 63 % admit to posting "for validation." – 100 % say "it's complicated." Economists define social media as **a zero-sum attention market powered by infinite insecurity.**

Epilogue Fragment: The Sign-Off

You stare at your phone one evening. You almost post something — a clever thought, a good photo, a small cry for relevance. Then you don't.

You close the app. Step outside. The air feels algorithm-free.

And for the first time in years, you're trending — at peace.

ARC IV: CONSUMPTION AND THE CONSUMER SELF

THE MARKET INSIDE YOUR MIND

CHAPTER XIX

IMPULSE PURCHASES AND BOUNDED RATIONALITY

Or: Kahneman meets the clearance aisle.

I. The Situation

You walk into a store to buy toothpaste. You emerge with a Bluetooth speaker, three scented candles, and a pair of slippers that promise “ergonomic mindfulness.” The toothpaste? Forgotten somewhere between “discounted quinoa” and “buy one, get one emotional void.”

At the checkout, you tell yourself it’s fine — “I deserved this.” You did. But so did your savings account.

Welcome to the **clearance aisle of human reason**, where decisions aren’t made — they’re *nudged.*

II. The Model: Bounded Rationality and the Shiny Object Hypothesis

Herbert Simon once proposed that humans aren’t perfectly rational decision-makers; we’re “satisficers” — we settle for good enough. Modern retailers heard that and replied, “Challenge accepted.”

Rational Model	Real-World Equivalent	Behavioral Outcome
Perfect Information	Knows all options	Clicks "Recommended For You"
Stable Preferences	Buys what's needed	Buys what's on sale
Utility Maximization	Optimizes value	Optimizes serotonin
Logical Consistency	Chooses deliberately	Panics under fluorescent lighting

This isn't irrationality. It's **bounded rationality** — thinking rationally within the narrow, candy-colored boundaries of temptation.

Retailers are simply *designing the boundaries.*

III. Anecdotal Case Study: The Checkout Gauntlet

Mehul just needed batteries. But the checkout line whispered temptations: chocolate bars, stress balls, and a keychain shaped like Baby Yoda. By the time he reached the cashier, he had accidentally built a small shrine to impulse.

Later, at home, he stared at the receipts. He couldn't recall *deciding* to buy any of it. That's because he didn't — *System 1* (Kahneman's fast, emotional brain) did.

System 2 arrived later, wearing the suit of justification:

"Well, I might need stress balls for work."

He now owns 11.

IV. The Behavioral Dynamics

Impulse buying is not chaos — it's choreography. Marketers conduct it with Pavlovian precision.

Key psychological biases in play:

- **Anchoring Bias:** The first price seen defines what "cheap" feels like.
- **Scarcity Effect:** "Only 2 left!" triggers survival mode.
- **Framing Effect:** "You save ₹100" feels better than "You spend ₹900."
- **Hyperbolic Discounting:** The promise of immediate joy outweighs distant regret.

In essence, every impulse buy is a small act of temporal betrayal — the present self mugging the future self in broad daylight.

V. Archetypes of the Impulse Buyer

Archetype	Core Strategy	Observable Behavior
The Optimistic Shopper	"I'll definitely use this!"	Doesn't.
The Emotional Buyer	Purchases feelings, not objects	Cries during unboxing
The Deal Hunter	Mistakes saving money for making money	Owns seven blenders
The Aspirational Minimalist	Buys books on decluttering	Never reads them
The Revenge Spender	"I've had a hard week."	Keeps having hard weeks

🗨 *Margin note:* "Impulse buying is retail's version of Tinder: low commitment, high regret, and someone always profits."

VI. The Strategic Takeaway: The Economics of Regret

Impulse purchasing reflects the **behavioral lag between want and reflection.** Rationally, we know the price of the product. Emotionally, we pay the premium of *dopamine now.*

In decision-theory terms:

Utility (U) = Immediate Satisfaction – Deferred Guilt.

Retailers optimize *U* by shortening guilt's arrival window — free shipping, instant checkout, "Buy Now Pay Later."

True strategic literacy means learning to slow that lag. If thinking fast is costly, thinking slowly is compound interest.

VII. Anecdote Two: The Midnight Cart Catastrophe

It's 11:47 p.m. *Priya* is "just browsing." She fills her cart with candles, notebooks, and an "anti-anxiety lamp." She doesn't check out — she just *likes knowing they're there.*

The next morning, the app sends a notification: *"Your cart misses you ♡ ."* She caves.

By noon, she's poorer but calmer — temporarily. This, behavioral economists note, is **purchase-induced placebo.**

VIII. The Corporate Parallel

Organizations commit impulse buys too — only with budgets instead of boredom. They chase "strategic initiatives," "digital transformations," or "innovative tools" that sounded good in the boardroom.

A new platform, a consultant, a "synergy dashboard." All justified under the sacred banner of "staying ahead."

In truth, it's the corporate version of a scented candle: smells smart, does nothing.

The difference between personal and corporate impulse? Zero. Only the receipts are longer.

IX. The Existential Undercurrent

Impulse buying isn't just about want — it's about *control.* For a fleeting moment, you're the sovereign of your micro-economy, making decisions unreviewed by bosses, partners, or society.

The tragedy is that every small act of rebellion comes prepackaged with a barcode. We shop not to own, but to *become* — briefly, the person who needed that object.

And when the high fades, we scroll again.

Because capitalism's greatest trick isn't selling things — it's selling second chances at selfhood.

X. The Moral (Receipt Length: Infinite)

Self-control is the most expensive item in the store.

Moral: Every impulse buy is a strategy failure disguised as self-care.

“Retail Psychology Index 2025”

Institute for Consumer Irrationality reports: – 79 % of online purchases are unplanned. – 61 % occur between 10 p.m. and 2 a.m. – 87 % of shoppers describe the feeling as “therapeutic.” Behavioral scientists classify impulse buying as **short-term hedonic optimization under chronic existential liquidity.**

Epilogue Fragment: The Drawer of Forgotten Things

Weeks later, you open a drawer and find something still wrapped in plastic — a relic of last month’s optimism. You smile, half in guilt, half in affection.

Then you think: *Maybe I’ll finally use this.* And the spiral begins again.

CHAPTER XX

SUBSCRIPTION OVERLOAD AS A DIVERSIFICATION FAILURE

> *Or: The tyranny of small recurring payments.*

I. The Situation

You used to *own* things. Now, you *subscribe* to them — music, movies, meals, meditation, fitness, and therapy (for the guilt caused by all of the above).

Your monthly credit card statement reads like a roll call of good intentions:

- Gym app (unused)
- Language learning app (abandoned at "Hola")
- Streaming service #4 ("just for that one show")
- Cloud storage you can't locate

Each charge looks harmless — ₹299 here, ₹199 there. Individually, they're manageable. Collectively, they're an *annuity of regret.*

Welcome to the **Subscription Singularity**, where commitment issues and financial decay meet in auto-renewal harmony.

II. The Model: Diversification Failure in Personal Portfolios

Finance textbooks teach us that **diversification spreads risk.** But in personal consumption, it often just spreads *forgetfulness.*

Principle	Rational Finance	Subscription Reality
Diversify across uncorrelated assets	Reduce volatility	Subscribe across identical apps
Monitor portfolio regularly	Ensure optimal allocation	Avoid opening "Manage Subscriptions"
Exit underperforming investments	Cut losses early	Forget password, surrender funds
Seek long-term growth	Compound wealth	Compound inertia

Thus, the modern consumer's portfolio resembles a confused hedge fund: 40 micro-investments in convenience, none delivering alpha.

We call this **The Diversification Fallacy.**

III. Anecdotal Case Study: The Streaming Spiral

Aditya once prided himself on "cutting cable to save money." He now pays for five streaming services — each with one exclusive show that "he'll get to eventually."

When he tried cancelling one, he was asked, "Are you sure? You'll lose access to *exclusive content.*" He stayed.

Six months later, he realized he'd spent ₹8,000 on *potential enjoyment.* Economists classify this as **subscription-based optimism bias.**

His true entertainment cost? Roughly ₹1,600 per watched episode.

IV. The Behavioral Dynamics

The subscription economy thrives on **temporal discounting** — our tendency to undervalue small, repeated costs relative to one large, visible one.

Biases that keep the cycle spinning:

- **The Pain of Paying Effect:** Small auto-charges dull our awareness.
- **Loss Aversion:** Cancelling feels like losing access, not saving money.
- **Endowment Effect:** Once we "have" a service, giving it up feels personal.
- **Hyperbolic Discounting:** Future regret is a poor deterrent for present convenience.

The true innovation of the subscription model wasn't technology — it was *psychological anesthesia.*

V. Archetypes of the Over-Subscribed

Archetype	Core Strategy	Observable Behavior
The Optimizer	Signs up "just to try"	Forgets to cancel trials
The Completionist	Must have every streaming platform	Watches nothing
The Delegator	"Family plan" for household peace	Nobody remembers who pays
The Productivity Addict	Subscribes to planners and focus apps	Still procrastinates

Archetype	Core Strategy	Observable Behavior
The Minimalist	Cancels everything	Eventually resubscribes "strategically"

🗨 *Margin note:* "Every cancelled subscription feels like moral progress. Until you realize you've subscribed to the idea of minimalism itself."

VI. The Strategic Takeaway: Attention Dilution and Cognitive Bandwidth

Each subscription consumes not just money, but *mental real estate.* It's portfolio bloat disguised as convenience.

In strategic terms:

Diversification without prioritization = diffusion.

We confuse abundance of access with abundance of value. But the real scarcity isn't content — it's attention. And attention, unlike money, can't be auto-renewed.

To paraphrase Peter Drucker (if he ever opened Netflix):

"What gets subscribed gets unmanaged."

VII. Anecdote Two: The Gym App that Never Dies

Ruchi downloaded a fitness app in 2020 — a lockdown experiment in self-improvement. She used it twice. Every month since, it charges ₹299 — quietly, faithfully, like a loyal ghost.

She once tried cancelling but couldn't find the option in the settings maze. When she emailed support, she got an automated reply: *"We're sorry to see you go."* She hadn't actually left.

Three years later, she calls it "my most stable relationship."

VIII. The Corporate Parallel

Companies, too, suffer **subscription creep.** Departments hoard SaaS tools, analytics dashboards, and "pilot programs" that nobody remembers authorizing. By fiscal year-end, half the tech stack exists purely out of inertia.

Finance calls it *"cost of convenience."* Culture calls it *"strategic alignment."* Reality calls it *"digital hoarding."*

The same behavioral trap applies: canceling feels like regression, even when it's optimization.

IX. The Existential Undercurrent

The subscription model monetizes our indecision. It transforms *maybe later* into a revenue stream. It thrives on guilt deferred and discipline postponed.

Somewhere deep down, we crave the illusion of readiness — the idea that access equals action. That having a subscription means becoming the kind of person who'll *use* it someday.

But that "someday" rarely arrives. Because, truthfully, we don't subscribe to services — we subscribe to *aspirations.*

X. The Moral (Auto-Renew On)

Convenience compounds faster than consciousness.

Moral: The smartest subscription you can cancel is the one to your own excuses.

"Subscription Economy 2025"

Institute for Behavioral Finance reports: – Average urban adult pays for 14 active subscriptions. – 60 % can't recall more than 8 of them. – 78 % experience "cancellation guilt." Economists define subscription overload as **recurring micro-irrationality bundled in monthly comfort.**

Epilogue Fragment: The Auto-Renew Moment

You get an email: *"Your plan has renewed successfully."* You sigh. You promise yourself you'll cancel next month.

You won't. But maybe — just maybe — you'll finally use it. And that, dear consumer, is the story of modern hope.

CHAPTER XXI

BRAND LOYALTY AND STOCKHOLM SYNDROME

> *Or: Emotional lock-in and cognitive dissonance.*

I. The Situation

You've been using the same phone brand for years. You defend it in arguments, ignore its flaws, and sneer at others' choices as if your device were a moral philosophy.

When it crashes, you blame yourself. When the competitor innovates, you call it gimmicky.

You, dear consumer, are no longer a customer. You're a **hostage with Stockholm Syndrome**—a willing captive who calls their captor "premium."

It's not a transaction anymore. It's a *relationship*. And like all relationships built on manipulation, it's expensive, co-dependent, and oddly comforting.

II. The Model: Emotional Lock-In Loop

Brand loyalty, once defined as repeat purchase behavior, has evolved into a psychological survival mechanism.

Phase	Emotional Mechanic	Observable Behavior	Strategic Term
1. Discovery	Novelty and validation	"This brand *gets* me."	Emotional differentiation

Phase	Emotional Mechanic	Observable Behavior	Strategic Term
2. Dependency	Comfort bias	"I can't switch now."	Switching cost
3. Rationalization	Cognitive dissonance	"They must have a good reason for this price."	Post-purchase justification
4. Evangelism	Identity projection	"You just don't *understand* the ecosystem."	Network defense
5. Entrapment	Resigned attachment	"Too late to start over."	Emotional lock-in

This loop sustains trillion-dollar empires. Because loyalty, once earned by value, is now extracted through *familiarity fatigue.*

III. Anecdotal Case Study: The Fruit Cult

Rhea has owned five consecutive smartphones from the same company—you know the one, symbolized by a fruit bitten just enough to suggest forbidden knowledge.

When asked why, she said:

"I like how it integrates with everything else I already have."

Translation:

"I'm trapped in an ecosystem so smooth it's practically a velvet prison."

Each new update feels mandatory. Each purchase feels ordained. When her phone battery began dying suspiciously fast, she Googled the issue—on her brand's own browser—and concluded it was "probably user error."

Her loyalty is indistinguishable from love.

Economists might call this **cognitive dissonance amortization.** Therapists might call it **codependency with push notifications.**

IV. The Behavioral Dynamics

Brands don't just sell products—they sell **narratives of belonging.**

Cognitive biases in play:

- **Endowment Effect:** Once you've invested, switching feels like loss.
- **Status Quo Bias:** Familiarity masquerades as safety.
- **Cognitive Dissonance:** You justify irrational loyalty to protect your self-image.
- **Social Identity Theory:** You're not just using the brand—you're *performing membership.*

The result: your brain mistakes branding for bonding.

V. Archetypes of the Loyal Captive

Archetype	Core Strategy	Observable Behavior
The Evangelist	Converts others	Speaks in slogans
The Historian	"I've used them since 2007."	Nostalgia as justification

Archetype	Core Strategy	Observable Behavior
The Investor	"Their products retain value."	Ignores depreciation
The Aesthetic Minimalist	"It just works."	Ignores when it doesn't
The Monogamist	"I don't cheat on my brands."	Treats alternatives as betrayal

🗨 *Margin note:* "At this stage, you don't need customer support. You need couples therapy."

VI. The Strategic Takeaway: When Preference Becomes Prison

In strategy terms, brand loyalty represents **a market inefficiency sustained by emotional inertia.**

The goal of marketing was once persuasion. Now it's **habituation**—training the consumer to *feel incomplete without you.*

Companies have replaced **price elasticity** with **psychological elasticity**—stretching your emotional tolerance until you call pain "premium."

The true strategist recognizes the line between trust and dependency:

If switching feels unthinkable, you're no longer a customer—you're an asset class.

VII. Anecdote Two: The Great Coffee Conversion

Dev, a proud aficionado of one global coffee chain, insisted it was "the best coffee in the world." He said this often, and always while waiting 12 minutes for his mobile order.

One day, his card failed. Forced into a nearby local café, he discovered something shocking: the coffee was better, cheaper, and came with eye contact.

He panicked. He felt *guilty.*

That's not caffeine withdrawal—it's brand betrayal guilt, a symptom of long-term identity colonization.

He now drinks both, telling himself, "I like variety." Denial is the first step toward freedom.

VIII. The Corporate Parallel

Organizations, too, suffer brand Stockholm Syndrome—only in reverse. They refuse to abandon legacy vendors, outdated systems, or consultants who last added value in the Obama era.

Internal rationale: "We've been partners for years." Actual meaning: "We're scared to learn something new."

In the same way individuals defend their brands, companies defend their mistakes—because change threatens continuity, and continuity feels like competence.

The result? Institutional inertia with a subscription plan.

IX. The Existential Undercurrent

At its heart, brand loyalty reveals our deeper longing: to belong somewhere stable, predictable, and aesthetically pleasing. The brand becomes our shorthand for identity.

We don't wear logos; we wear **certificates of existence.** We don't upgrade devices; we renew belief systems.

Capitalism has quietly outsourced religion—not to temples or churches, but to flagship stores with minimalist interiors and gospel pricing.

Our saints are influencers. Our hymns are jingles. Our confessions are product reviews.

And our prayers? "Please fix it in the next update."

X. The Moral (Warranty Expired)

The line between love and loyalty is a fine print no one reads.

Moral: When your identity depends on your brand, customer support becomes confession.

"Consumer Attachment Report 2025"

Institute for Behavioral Branding reports: – 71 % of consumers feel "emotionally connected" to at least one brand. – 54 % describe that connection as "complicated." – 27 % admit they'd rather switch partners than phones. Behavioral economists define brand loyalty as **voluntary captivity with recurring billing.**

Epilogue Fragment: The Upgrade Cycle

The new model releases tomorrow. You tell yourself you don't need it. Then you see the ad: *"It's not an upgrade. It's you, evolved."*

You sigh, smile, and pre-order. Because freedom, after all, is just a different color option.

CHAPTER XXII

DECISION FATIGUE IN FOOD DELIVERY

Or: Choice architecture and algorithmic manipulation.

I. The Situation

It's 8:37 p.m. You've had a long day, a low battery, and a high stress index. You open your food delivery app, and are greeted by an endless scroll of options: 2,000 restaurants, 27 cuisines, 41 "exclusive deals," and a popup reminding you that your "favorites are just a tap away."

Twenty-three minutes later, you're still scrolling. You're hungry, but also oddly detached — like a monk meditating in a neon bazaar.

Eventually, you order *the same thing as last time*. Because sometimes, even surrender is a strategy.

This is not indecision. This is **algorithmic exhaustion**—the silent killer of modern appetite.

II. The Model: The Decision Fatigue Curve

Psychologist Roy Baumeister defined decision fatigue as the *depletion of cognitive energy through repeated choice-making.* In other words, every "What should I eat?" silently consumes willpower units.

Phase	Choices Made	Cognitive Load	Behavioral Outcome
1. Morning (Optimistic)	Low	Light	"I'll have oats."
2. Afternoon (Distracted)	Medium	Moderate	"Maybe a salad… or not."
3. Evening (Depleted)	High	Severe	"Whatever's fastest."
4. Late Night (Gone)	Infinite	None left	"Cheese fries are self-care."

The result: *choice paralysis* followed by *regret optimization.*

Economists call it **bounded rationality.** Marketers call it **customer engagement.** You call it **Tuesday night.**

III. Anecdotal Case Study: The Menu Maze

Anuj opens his app to order dinner. He filters by "fast delivery," then "best rating," then "new restaurants," then "offers." He's now cross-filtered himself into a paradox:

"Top-rated new places offering fast discounts that deliver before 9."

The app cheerfully shows **zero results.**

So he resets filters and orders from "Recently Ordered." The irony? The algorithm had predicted this 17 minutes ago.

That's not coincidence — that's *predictive conditioning.* Anuj isn't choosing dinner. Dinner is choosing him.

IV. The Behavioral Dynamics

Food delivery platforms are masterclasses in **choice architecture** — the subtle art of shaping decisions without appearing to.

Cognitive biases exploited include:

- **Choice Overload Effect:** More options reduce satisfaction.
- **Default Bias:** Users tend to reorder the familiar.
- **Recency Effect:** Last-seen restaurants feel more appealing.
- **Anchoring:** "Top-rated" sets the reference frame for all else.
- **Personalization Illusion:** "Recommended for you" is often "profitable for us."

The real menu isn't on your screen; it's in your *data profile.* You are not the customer — you are the experiment.

V. Archetypes of the Fatigued Feeder

Archetype	Core Strategy	Observable Behavior
The Scroller	Endless browsing	Eats after hunger dies
The Loyalist	Reorders same dish	Calls it "consistency"
The Gambler	"Let's try something new!"	Complains about it later
The Optimizer	Applies five filters	Ends up in paradox
The Existentialist	"What's the point?"	Closes app, skips dinner

Margin note: "Indecision is the modern diet."

VI. The Strategic Takeaway: The Tyranny of Micro-Freedom

Decision fatigue reveals the hidden flaw in consumer capitalism — the myth that *more choice = more happiness.*

But abundance is not freedom; it's **cognitive tax.** Every extra option incurs mental processing cost without necessarily increasing satisfaction.

In strategy terms:

Choice optimization without cognitive budget leads to strategic burnout.

Thus, the most successful modern businesses aren't the ones offering the most options — but the ones offering **the illusion of choice with the comfort of certainty.** (*"Your usual?"* is now a UX feature, not a question.)

VII. Anecdote Two: The Algorithm Always Wins

Nikita noticed her delivery app always recommended one specific pasta joint. Curious, she resisted it for a week.

By Day 5, the app sent her a notification: *"Craving your favorite?"* By Day 6, she caved. By Day 7, it offered her a coupon "as a reward for loyalty."

She felt accomplished — until she realized she had been rewarded for *predictability.*

Behavioral scientists call this **reinforcement learning.** Philosophers might call it **fate with push notifications.**

VIII. The Corporate Parallel

Organizations face their own decision fatigue — too many initiatives, too many dashboards, too many "strategic priorities."

By quarter's end, leaders do what consumers do: revert to what's safe, measurable, and familiar.

Thus, "innovation" quietly loops back to "whatever worked last year." The company, like the hungry user, mistakes exhaustion for efficiency.

In both cases, **choice becomes camouflage for control.**

IX. The Existential Undercurrent

We order food not just to eat, but to outsource the burden of deciding. It's not hunger that drives the click — it's fatigue masquerading as appetite.

The tragedy of convenience is that it replaces thought with automation, and then charges us for the subscription.

Every algorithmic nudge whispers the same seduction:

"Don't think. Just tap."

And each tap feels liberating — until you realize you've traded autonomy for ease.

X. The Moral (Estimated Delivery: 32 Minutes)

When the menu expands, meaning contracts.

Moral: Freedom without focus is just another notification.

> **"Cognitive Load Index 2025"**
>
> *Institute for Behavioral Nutrition reports:* – Average user spends 19 minutes choosing meals online. – 63 % reorder from "recently ordered." – 82 % experience "mild regret" post-meal. Behavioral economists define this as **algorithmic consumption under decision scarcity.**

Epilogue Fragment: The Reorder Button

The next night, you don't browse. You just tap "Reorder."

The food arrives faster. You feel efficient. You've optimized away choice itself.

Outside, the world still offers infinite cuisines. Inside, you're just hungry for silence.

CHAPTER XXIII

SUSTAINABILITY SIGNALING

Or: Virtue as currency in the moral marketplace.

I. The Situation

You stand in a supermarket aisle holding two coffee brands:

- One claims to be "100% ethically sourced, carbon neutral, and rainforest positive."
- The other just says "coffee."

You hesitate. Not because of taste or price — but because one of them might make you look like a bad person.

You choose the ethical one. You feel good. You post about it. You never check where it actually came from.

Congratulations: you've successfully completed a **moral transaction.** It's not consumption anymore — it's *self-reputation management.*

II. The Model: The Virtue Signaling Supply Chain

Modern consumption operates in two layers:

1. **Functional value** — what the product does.
2. **Moral value** — what it *says about you.*

Step	Input	Output	Cognitive Benefit
1. Product Design	Eco-friendly adjectives	Emotional reassurance	Guilt offset

Step	Input	Output	Cognitive Benefit
2. Consumer Choice	"Conscious selection"	Moral self-signal	Identity validation
3. Public Display	Instagram post, tote bag	Social approval	Virtue ROI
4. Forgetfulness	Cognitive closure	Emotional reset	Room for next purchase

Economists call this **value stacking** — every item carries both utility and morality. Philosophers might call it **gentrified guilt management.**

III. Anecdotal Case Study: The Bamboo Toothbrush Revolution

Ritika decided to live "sustainably." She bought bamboo toothbrushes, metal straws, reusable grocery bags, and an expensive composting bin that she used twice.

Her electricity still came from coal, and her SUV still had three air fresheners, but the toothbrush made her feel *balanced.*

When asked why she switched, she said,

"I just want to do my bit."

That "bit," economists note, cost ₹499 and came wrapped in three layers of biodegradable guilt.

Behavioral scientists call this **moral licensing** — the tendency to commit small good deeds to justify larger indulgences.

IV. The Behavioral Dynamics

Sustainability signaling thrives on three psychological levers:

1. **The Halo Effect:** One visible ethical act (e.g., carrying a canvas bag) makes you *feel* broadly virtuous.
2. **Cognitive Dissonance Reduction:** Ethical consumption soothes the unease of being part of the problem.
3. **Identity Economics:** We buy not just to own, but to *be seen as a certain kind of person.*

The real product isn't the thing — it's the **narrative of responsibility.** You're not purchasing soap; you're purchasing a belief that your soap is fighting climate change while you shower.

V. Archetypes of the Conscious Consumer

Archetype	Core Strategy	Observable Behavior
The Eco Evangelist	Converts friends	Cites documentaries nobody watched
The Token Minimalist	Buys fewer things, but pricier ones	Calls it "intentional living"
The Carbon Accountant	Tracks every offset	Books flights anyway
The Tote Bag Collector	Owns 15 "reusable" bags	Forgets them every time
The Sincerity Skeptic	Buys local, distrusts everyone	Exhausted, but smugly correct

🗨 *Margin note:* "Sustainability is the art of feeling eco-positive while driving a 4,000-pound guilt chariot."

VI. The Strategic Takeaway: Virtue as a Market Differentiator

In corporate strategy, sustainability began as compliance. Then it became differentiation. Now it's **brand theology**.

The key insight:

In a world of moral inflation, virtue becomes the new premium.

Brands no longer compete on price or performance — they compete on righteousness. Carbon-neutral, cruelty-free, gender-inclusive, gluten-sensitive — each a badge in the Olympics of Optics.

The more guilt they can absorb on your behalf, the higher they can price it.

VII. Anecdote Two: The Recycled Redemption

Kabir, a self-professed sustainability warrior, once spent ₹3,200 on a limited-edition "recycled ocean plastic" jacket. When it arrived, it looked identical to his old polyester one.

He wore it proudly — until he realized it was *shipped individually by air from Denmark.*

When asked if he felt misled, he said,

"At least I'm part of the solution."

In reality, he was part of the *marketing department's solution.*

Economists call this **greenwashing.** Kabir calls it *hope, slightly overpriced.*

VIII. The Corporate Parallel

Organizations mirror the same pattern: ESG reports as performance theatre, sustainability dashboards that glow greener than the forests they cite.

They hire Chief Impact Officers, release "net-zero by 2035" pledges, and hold internal events where paper straws are served in plastic cups.

It's not strategy — it's **optical equilibrium:** the delicate balancing of moral ambition and market apathy.

Somewhere in the PowerPoint decks of the world, a single tree graphic has offset 200 tons of emissions.

IX. The Existential Undercurrent

We crave moral coherence in a world that rewards convenience. And when real change feels too slow or systemic, symbolic virtue becomes a proxy for agency.

Buying "ethical" gives us permission to keep participating — to be both *complicit and comforted.*

In truth, sustainability signaling is less about saving the planet and more about saving face. It's not hypocrisy; it's *coping.* The modern condition: guilty, informed, and subscribed to newsletters about both.

X. The Moral (Compost in Progress)

Conscience is the new commodity — endlessly renewable, easily marketed.

Moral: When virtue becomes a product, redemption goes on sale.

"The Green Economy, 2025"

Institute for Sustainable Consumerism reports: – 68 % of consumers will pay more for "ethical" products. – 71 % can't define "ethical." – 89 % say "it makes them feel better." Behavioral economists define this as **transactional virtue optimization with selective memory.**

Epilogue Fragment: The Biodegradable Epiphany

You sip from your reusable water bottle while ordering fast fashion online. A pop-up asks, *"Add ₹10 to plant a tree?"* You click yes.

Somewhere, a spreadsheet gets greener. You sleep well. And the planet spins on — sustainably bewildered.

CHAPTER XXIV

MINIMALISM AS A MAXIMALIST STRATEGY

> *Or: Strategic simplicity and conspicuous restraint.*

I. The Situation

You stand in your newly decluttered living room. White walls. One plant (thriving, of course). A single chair made of recycled oak that cost roughly the GDP of Bhutan.

You feel light, serene, and vaguely superior — until you realize your old "non-essential" belongings are now taking up space in someone else's garage.

You post a photo with the caption: *"Learning to live with less 🙏."* The post performs well.

Minimalism has never looked so… full.

II. The Model: Strategic Simplicity as Market Differentiation

Traditional economics assumes that *more* consumption indicates *greater* wealth. Modern signaling theory suggests the opposite: *true affluence lies in visible restraint.*

Consumption Style	External Signal	Strategic Analogy
Maximalist	"I can afford more."	Market share dominance
Minimalist	"I can afford not to."	Strategic focus
Ascetic	"I've transcended need."	Market exit
Conflicted	"I buy minimalism books."	Brand confusion

In other words, minimalism isn't about owning less — it's about **curating scarcity.** The fewer things you own, the more narrative each thing must carry.

III. Anecdotal Case Study: The Capsule Wardrobe Conundrum

Ananya decided to "simplify her life" after reading an article titled *"The Joy of Less."* She donated half her clothes, kept ten versatile pieces, and immediately bought a linen shirt from a boutique that described itself as "sustainably minimal."

Within a month, she owned four such shirts.

When asked about the contradiction, she said:

"It's not about owning less — it's about owning *better.*"

Behavioral economists call this **curated consumption.** Sociologists call it **luxury laundering.** Her accountant calls it *unchanged.*

IV. The Behavioral Dynamics

Minimalism preys on **decision fatigue** and **status anxiety**, packaging relief as philosophy.

Key psychological levers include:

- **Cognitive Load Reduction:** Simplicity feels like control.
- **Identity Consolidation:** "I am the kind of person who doesn't need much."
- **Moral Licensing:** Owning fewer things justifies owning pricier things.
- **Social Signaling:** Simplicity becomes a form of social capital.

In short: minimalism is capitalism's soft reboot — same operating system, cleaner interface.

V. Archetypes of the Modern Minimalist

Archetype	Core Strategy	Observable Behavior
The Aesthetic Monk	Lives in grayscale	Owns candles labeled "void"
The Functionalist	"Everything has a purpose."	Collects storage boxes
The Digital Minimalist	Deletes social media	Announces it online
The Eco-Minimalist	Buys bamboo everything	Still shops monthly
The Meta-Minimalist	Rejects minimalism merch	Blogs about it weekly

🗨 *Margin note:* "Nothing says simplicity like a $120 minimalist journal titled '*Less.*'"

VI. The Strategic Takeaway: Subtraction as Positioning

In corporate strategy, simplicity is a *competitive moat.* Fewer products, clearer choices, stronger identity. The same applies to personal brands.

Focus is the new extravagance.

Minimalism, then, isn't an anti-consumer stance — it's a **rebranding of consumption as mindfulness.** You don't stop buying; you *curate acquisitions with philosophical flair.*

Luxury brands caught on early: the same handbag, but "reinterpreted through essentialist design." The result: maximal profit from minimal material.

Minimalism, in other words, is the **Apple-ization of asceticism.**

VII. Anecdote Two: The Great Decluttering Cascade

Rahul watched a documentary about tidying up. Inspired, he threw away 40% of his possessions — including a perfectly good set of plates because "they didn't spark joy." Two days later, he realized he had nothing to eat on. He bought a new minimalist set: matte finish, artisanal, ₹3,999.

When asked how it felt, he said:

"Peaceful, but expensive."

Economists classify this under **the decluttering paradox** — where the cost of simplicity exceeds the chaos it replaces.

VIII. The Corporate Parallel

Businesses, too, fetishize minimalism. Rebranding as "lean," "agile," or "flat," they shed middle managers and legacy systems — only to replace them with consulting subscriptions and frameworks describing how "less is more."

Minimalism at scale becomes **strategic austerity** — simplicity for the consumer, complexity for the supplier.

A company that preaches "focus" often just can't afford the alternative.

The boardroom moral mirrors the bedroom: when you can't manage clutter, call it design.

IX. The Existential Undercurrent

Minimalism's real allure isn't aesthetic — it's existential. In a world of noise, simplicity feels like control. But beneath the calm veneer lies a quiet anxiety: if we strip away everything, will anything meaningful remain?

The minimalist doesn't reject possessions — they fear irrelevance. Their spaces are empty not because they're detached, but because they're desperate for clarity in a world oversupplied with meaning.

Minimalism isn't rebellion; it's retreat. A power nap in the midst of capitalism's never-ending sprint.

X. The Moral (Clean Lines, Messy Minds)

Simplicity sells best to those drowning in complexity.

Moral: Minimalism isn't about having less — it's about *having less to apologize for.*

"Minimalism Market Index, 2025"

Institute for Lifestyle Economics reports: – 62 % of minimalists describe themselves as "recovering consumers." – 48 % spend more on "quality" goods than before decluttering. – 91 % say their life feels calmer — 67 % can't explain why. Economists define minimalism as **conspicuous restraint under aesthetic inflation.**

Epilogue Fragment: The Empty Shelf

You stand before your pristine, decluttered shelf. It looks beautiful, purposeful, serene.

Then you wonder — should you get a book about minimalism to complete the look? You smile. You open your laptop.

And just like that, the cycle begins anew — clean, curated, and quietly chaotic.

ARC V: THE RELATIONSHIP ECONOMY

LOVE, LEVERAGE, AND LOSS LEADERS

CHAPTER XXV

DATING APPS AS MULTI-SIDED MARKETS

Or: Network effects and asymmetric information.

I. The Situation

You download a dating app. You upload your best photo — the one from three summers ago, when your lighting and optimism were both better. You write a bio: short, witty, vaguely profound (*"Fluent in sarcasm and small joys 🌿"*).

Then you swipe. And swipe. And swipe.

Each match feels like possibility; each silence feels like market failure. It's exhilarating, exhausting, and existentially expensive.

Because you're not just searching for love — you're participating in **a real-time auction for attention.**

II. The Model: Multi-Sided Market Dynamics

A *multi-sided market* connects two or more distinct user groups that provide value to each other through the platform. In dating apps, the groups are:

- **Users A:** People seeking connection.
- **Users B:** People also seeking connection (the same group, inconveniently).
- **Platform C:** The intermediary, monetizing uncertainty.

Stakeholder	Objective	Strategy	Value Capture
Users	Find compatibility	Optimize self-presentation	Emotional ROI
Platform	Maximize engagement	Engineer scarcity	Subscription revenue
Advertisers	Sell aspiration	Leverage intimacy data	Precision targeting

It's not a love story. It's a **two-sided liquidity problem with identity constraints.**

III. Anecdotal Case Study: The Swipe Economy

Rohit joined three dating apps "to maximize reach." He crafted tailored bios for each:

- App A: "Looking for something real."
- App B: "Here for a good conversation."
- App C: "Just exploring!"

By Day 12, he had 64 matches — and zero actual plans.

The paradox: **abundance without access.** Each potential connection was trapped in a loop of polite banter and slow ghosting — a liquidity glut in the love market.

He didn't delete the apps; he *reinvested.* Bought premium. Boosted visibility. Still no ROI.

Economists would call this **the paradox of choice under asymmetric attention.**

Rohit calls it *Tuesday.*

IV. The Behavioral Dynamics

Dating apps thrive on **asymmetric information** — the gap between who you are and how you're represented.

Cognitive biases exploited include:

- **Signaling Bias:** Attractive photos act as visual currencies.
- **Anchoring Effect:** The first impression (photo, tagline) defines perceived worth.
- **Reciprocity Illusion:** A "match" feels mutual — it's just algorithmic pairing.
- **FOMO Loop:** Each swipe is a lottery ticket; stopping feels like missing out.

Every match isn't validation — it's *engagement time.* Love may be blind, but the algorithm is not.

V. Archetypes in the Dating Marketplace

Archetype	Market Behavior	Strategic Weakness
The Optimizer	Treats dating as analytics	Suffers data fatigue
The Dreamer	Waits for "chemistry"	Rejects 98 % of reality
The Serial Sampler	High churn rate	Low conversion
The Profile Curator	Spends hours editing	Forgets to reply
The Existential Scroller	"Just seeing what's out there"	Forgets what they're looking for

🗨 *Margin note:* "Swiping is the new prayer — repetitive, hopeful, unanswered."

VI. The Strategic Takeaway: Platform-Engineered Dependency

In strategic terms, dating apps operate on **engineered inefficiency.** They must deliver enough connection to sustain hope, but not enough satisfaction to end usage.

A perfect match is anti-revenue.

Hence, the platforms optimize *search*, not *success*. Their business model relies on the same principle as casinos and social media: *variable reward schedules.*

Each swipe delivers a dopamine possibility — intermittent, unpredictable, addictive. Love becomes gamified. Intimacy becomes interface.

VII. Anecdote Two: The Ghost in the Machine

Nisha met *Aarav* on an app. They chatted for weeks — witty, consistent, emotionally literate. When she finally suggested meeting, he vanished.

Days later, she realized his last message had been sent *after* his profile disappeared.

Aarav wasn't ghosting. He was part of an A/B test for engagement timing — the platform had archived his account mid-experiment.

In the algorithm's eyes, both were active data points. In human terms: one heartbreak, two clicks, zero accountability.

VIII. The Corporate Parallel

Organizations mimic dating apps when managing talent, partners, or customers. They optimize *matching metrics* but neglect *relational maintenance.*

Recruitment platforms chase click-through rates instead of cultural fit. Consultancies "speed-date" clients with glossy decks and shallow chemistry. Everyone's swiping right on synergy — no one's staying for substance.

The boardroom takeaway:

"Engagement" isn't the same as "connection." Most businesses, like dating apps, monetize the space between.

IX. The Existential Undercurrent

Dating apps promise efficiency — the idea that technology can algorithm our way into intimacy. But love isn't logistics; it's entropy.

We outsource vulnerability to interfaces, outsource conversation to emojis, outsource rejection to silence. We're optimizing ourselves out of the very awkwardness that makes connection *human.*

The result: a paradoxical loneliness — surrounded by potential partners, yet starved of presence. The tragedy isn't that love has become a marketplace. It's that we've mistaken *matching* for *meeting.*

X. The Moral (Swipe Left, Think Right)

Every profile is a hypothesis. Every swipe, a bet on probability disguised as fate.

Moral: You can't find "the one" when your strategy is built on infinite options.

"Dating Economy 2025"

Institute for Relational Economics reports: – 75 % of dating app users describe it as "exhausting but necessary." – 61 % admit to using multiple platforms simultaneously. – 42 % say they've "fallen for someone's profile, not the person." Economists define modern dating as **a two-sided attention market sustained by emotional liquidity.**

Epilogue Fragment: The Swipe Hangover

You close the app for the night. You promise yourself you'll "take a break." Tomorrow, a new notification pings: *"Someone likes you."*

You smile. You open it. The market reopens.

CHAPTER XXVI

THE FIRST DATE PITCH DECK

Or: Storytelling, framing, and customer conversion.

I. The Situation

It's 7:29 p.m. You're sitting at a café that smells of roasted confidence and artisanal nerves.

Your date is late by seven minutes — the acceptable window between fashionably delayed and mildly concerning. You've checked your reflection in your phone thrice, adjusted your smile twice, and revised your talking points once.

And that's when you realize: this isn't a date. It's a **pitch meeting.**

You're about to sell the most overvalued, under-tested product on the market: *yourself.*

II. The Model: The First Date as a Conversion Funnel

Let's be honest — dating is **customer acquisition with hormones.**

Funnel Stage	Objective	Tactical Behavior	Common KPI
Awareness	Establish brand recall	Be memorable without trauma	Eye contact ratio

Funnel Stage	Objective	Tactical Behavior	Common KPI
Consideration	Build curiosity	Tell stories with plausible humility	"That's interesting." count
Conversion	Secure next meeting	Close gracefully	Text follow-up time (in hours)

Your date, meanwhile, is running a parallel funnel. It's a **two-way due diligence process** disguised as banter about music and travel.

The stakes? A second round of both drinks and decisions.

III. Anecdotal Case Study: The Elevator Pitch Gone Awry

Rhea went on a first date with *Kabir*, a consultant (because of course). Kabir opened with, "So tell me about yourself," then proceeded to spend the next 23 minutes doing exactly that.

By the time he got to his "passion for meaningful impact," Rhea had mentally exited the meeting.

His pitch deck was well-rehearsed — just poorly audience-tested.

The takeaway: **information asymmetry doesn't equal intrigue.** She didn't ghost him; she simply unsubscribed.

IV. The Behavioral Dynamics

First dates operate on the principles of **framing, storytelling, and controlled disclosure.**

Psychological biases at play:

- **Anchoring Effect:** The first impression dominates the rest of the interaction.
- **Framing Bias:** Context defines perception — "ambitious" sounds better than "workaholic."
- **The Spotlight Effect:** You think your every move is being judged; in reality, your date is too busy worrying about theirs.
- **Confirmation Bias:** People notice what fits their pre-decided narrative — your date might already have an image of you built from emojis.

Every smile, anecdote, and self-deprecating quip becomes a **slide** in your implicit presentation. You are pitching *"Why Me: A Case for Limited Monogamy."*

V. Archetypes in the Dating Pitch

Archetype	**Presentation Strategy**	**Conversion Risk**
The Storyteller	Relies on narrative charm	Overshares Act II trauma
The Consultant	Uses jargon ("alignment", "synergy")	Treats date as QBR
The Philosopher	"What even *is* connection?"	Lost in abstraction
The Comedian	Wins laughs, loses depth	Becomes entertainment, not investment
The Minimalist	Says little, listens much	Perceived as mysterious, or bored

🗨 *Margin Note:* "Every first date is a product launch — except the product hasn't been QA-tested, and the audience might be allergic."

VI. The Strategic Framework: Framing as Market Positioning

In brand strategy, **framing defines value.** You're not selling what you are; you're selling how you're perceived.

Attraction = Authenticity × (Confidence ÷ Oversharing).

This equation, while unscientific, holds across multiple domains of both romance and marketing.

- **Brand Storytelling:** Replace "user journeys" with "personal growth arcs."
- **Unique Value Proposition:** Distill your quirks into memorable soundbites ("I once got locked inside a library — long story.")
- **Social Proof:** References from friends, anecdotes of kindness, casual mentions of pets.
- **Scarcity Principle:** Subtle cues of independence — because nothing says value like *unavailability.*

VII. Anecdote Two: The Investor Who Said "Maybe"

Arjun went on a date with *Leah*, an art curator. He opened strong: humor, warmth, well-fitted shirt.

By dessert, he'd delivered a perfect pitch deck — clear mission ("seeking something real"), compelling USP ("emotionally available, gainfully employed"), and an irresistible call to action ("Would love to see you again").

Leah smiled, said, "Let's stay in touch," and vanished into the ether of polite rejection.

He'd mistaken interest for intent — a **classic investor fallacy.**

Sometimes, the customer nods not because they'll buy — but because they respect the effort.

VIII. The Corporate Parallel

The boardroom is littered with first-date logic. Founders oversell vision, understate volatility, and charm investors with rehearsed authenticity.

Like dating, it's a dance of **impression management under time constraints.** You can't reveal too much risk, nor appear too polished.

The best pitches — romantic or professional — blend clarity with vulnerability. You don't just sell features; you sell *future stories.*

Both rely on the same strategic illusion: that *alignment* today will translate into *synergy* tomorrow.

IX. The Existential Undercurrent

First dates reveal our truest contradiction: we crave honesty, but reward presentation. We say we want authenticity — but only the curated kind.

Modern love is a PowerPoint presentation with human emotions. We evaluate, benchmark, and forecast compatibility — and then blame "chemistry" when the model fails.

Somewhere between risk mitigation and emotional ROI, romance became a corporate function.

We aren't courting — we're onboarding.

X. The Moral (Closing Slide with a Smile)

In the pitch of life, every date is an investor meeting — and every "let's catch up again" is a soft commitment, not a signed term sheet.

Moral: Love isn't about selling your best version — it's about surviving the due diligence.

"First Date Conversion Metrics, 2025"

Institute for Romantic Analytics reports: – 57 % of first dates are described as "fine." – 38 % lead to a second meeting. – 5 % lead to something lasting. – 100 % involve overthinking. Behavioral economists define first dates as **high-risk, low-data interactions with significant reputational exposure.**

Epilogue Fragment: The Follow-Up Email

You wake up the next morning. You type, delete, and retype a message that sounds casual but not careless.

Finally, you send: *"Had a lovely evening — would love to meet again sometime ☺."* Then you wait.

No reply yet. You tell yourself it's fine. You open the app again.

The market, once more, is open for business.

CHAPTER XXVII

RELATIONSHIP PORTFOLIO MANAGEMENT

Or: Diversification, risk appetite, and exit options.

I. The Situation

It begins, as all investments do, with optimism.

You meet someone. They're funny, charming, emotionally literate (or at least they text in full sentences). Your heart — that reckless venture capitalist — immediately commits **all available capital**.

You ignore due diligence. You assume infinite returns. You tell your friends, *"This one feels different."* They nod, the way seasoned investors do when they've seen this market before.

Weeks later, the volatility begins. Their messages slow. Your expectations rise. You start "diversifying emotionally" — not out of strategy, but survival.

Welcome to **portfolio management for the romantically leveraged.**

II. The Model: The Emotional Investment Portfolio

Every relationship portfolio contains a mix of assets:

Asset Class	Description	Risk Level	Typical Return
High-Volatility Crush	Intense attraction, unstable fundamentals	Very High	Sudden existential clarity
Mid-Cap Relationship	Moderate commitment, decent liquidity	Medium	Emotional growth, recurring drama
Legacy Connection	Long-term bond, low exit flexibility	Low	Stability, routine dividends
Speculative Flirtation	Minimal investment, high optionality	High	Entertainment yield

The optimal portfolio, of course, depends on one's **risk appetite** — a polite way of asking how much heartbreak your ego can afford.

Behavioral finance calls this **emotional diversification.** Therapists call it *avoidance.*

III. Anecdotal Case Study: The Overexposed Investor

Neha fell for *Dev* within three weeks. They were inseparable, symbiotic, and insufferable to their friends.

But Dev, sensing overvaluation, "needed space."

Neha responded by holding on longer — convinced that the market would correct itself. She waited, texted occasionally, and reread old messages for dividend reassurance.

Three months later, she finally admitted:

"I was emotionally overweighted in one asset."

Economists would classify this as **loss aversion** — the inability to exit a declining position because the loss feels too personal.

IV. The Behavioral Dynamics

Relationships mirror financial portfolios because both are governed by irrational psychology:

- **Overconfidence Bias:** "I can fix them."
- **Endowment Effect:** "But we have history."
- **Sunk Cost Fallacy:** "I've already invested so much time."
- **Availability Heuristic:** "They texted me once last week — things are improving."

We don't manage love rationally; we manage it narratively. We don't track performance; we *interpret volatility as depth.*

Love, it turns out, is the original high-beta asset class.

V. Archetypes of Relationship Investors

Archetype	Strategy	Risk Profile	Common Failure Mode
The Serial Diversifier	Multiple small emotional bets	High churn	Shallow returns
The Long-Term Holder	Commits early, resists rebalancing	Moderate	Stagnation
The Opportunistic Re-Entry	Revisits old investments	High	Nostalgia bubble
The Contrarian	Falls for the unavailable	Catastrophic	Identity loss
The Risk-Averse Skeptic	Avoids all new exposure	Minimal	Emotional illiquidity

Margin note: "Emotional diversification sounds wise until you realize you're benchmarking affection."

VI. The Strategic Framework: Love as Risk Management

Every mature relationship operates on three pillars:

1. **Liquidity** — How easily can you express needs, adapt, and recover?
2. **Correlation Risk** — Are both partners affected by the same stressors (work, mood, Netflix password)?
3. **Diversification** — Are you cultivating friendships, hobbies, and identities outside the relationship?

An over-concentrated portfolio (read: "You're my everything") is beautiful in poetry, disastrous in practice. Healthy portfolios balance intimacy with independence — emotional hedging disguised as self-care.

VII. Anecdote Two: The Great Rebalancing

Arnav had been in a three-year relationship that plateaued somewhere between comfort and confusion. When asked if he was happy, he said,

"It's fine. It's… stable."

He treated his relationship like a bond — predictable yields, low volatility. Until one day, his partner announced she was "reassessing her personal growth strategy."

He was shocked, despite the obvious market signals.

In retrospect, Arnav realized he'd forgotten to **rebalance.** What began as a growth fund had turned into a low-interest account.

Sometimes stability isn't safety — it's stagnation.

VIII. The Corporate Parallel

Corporate relationships — mergers, partnerships, alliances — follow the same cycle:

- Euphoric synergy forecasts.
- Integration fatigue.
- Value erosion.
- Exit planning disguised as "strategic review."

The emotional equivalent: early passion, mid-term maintenance, late-stage inertia.

Successful partnerships — corporate or romantic — depend less on alignment at the start, and more on **agility during drift.**

Love, like business, is less about returns and more about *liquidity management under uncertainty.*

IX. The Existential Undercurrent

We seek "the one" as if love were a monopoly market — when in truth, it's an ecosystem of shifting investments. No one person can fulfill every emotional need; the healthiest relationships outsource parts of themselves — to friends, passions, solitude.

But modern romance frames diversification as disloyalty. We confuse *focus* with *fulfillment.*

Perhaps the trick isn't to find perfect compatibility, but to manage imperfect portfolios gracefully — accepting periodic losses without liquidating the entire fund.

X. The Moral (Love's Quarterly Report)

Love, like any market, rewards those who review, rebalance, and occasionally cut losses before insolvency.

Moral: In relationships as in finance, diversification isn't disinterest — it's survival.

"The Emotional Index, 2025"

Institute for Relational Economics reports: – 68 % of adults describe their relationships as "emotionally stable but growth-limited." – 47 % maintain "side investments" in the form of close friendships or secret playlists. – 22 % admit to "checking the market value" of exes periodically. Behavioral economists define love as **a high-volatility emotional asset with no guaranteed dividends and infinite rollover clauses.**

Epilogue Fragment: The Exit Clause

You scroll through old photos, debating whether to delete or archive. You don't. Not yet.

Some investments, you tell yourself, are worth keeping — if only as a reminder of what not to overleverage next time.

You close the album, make tea, and whisper to no one in particular: "Maybe it's time to rebalance."

CHAPTER XXVIII

MARITAL NEGOTIATIONS

> *Or: Win-win, BATNA, and why "sleeping on the couch" is a reversion strategy.*

I. The Situation

Marriage begins, like all mergers, with synergy slides and overoptimistic forecasts. Two entities combine assets (love, playlists, Netflix passwords) and promise operational harmony.

Then, within six months, the integration challenges begin.

You discover incompatible workflows:

- Different sleep schedules.
- Conflicting definitions of "clean."
- Irreconcilable thermostat preferences.

Suddenly, the marriage isn't just a romance — it's an *ongoing negotiation between two sovereign states with nuclear capability and shared laundry baskets.*

II. The Model: The Household as a Negotiation Table

Marital equilibrium, like economic equilibrium, doesn't mean harmony — it means **mutual exhaustion at compatible levels.**

Negotiation Phase	Typical Trigger	Tactics Employed	Probable Outcome
Initial Bargaining	"Where do we eat tonight?"	Anchoring, selective listening	Mutual resentment masked as choice
Midterm Review	"You always do this."	Historical referencing	Emotional inflation
Crisis Summit	"We need to talk."	Escalation to agenda items	Rebalancing or stalemate
Resolution	"Let's just drop it."	Face-saving compromise	Temporary peace treaty

The central dynamic here is *BATNA* — the **Best Alternative to a Negotiated Agreement.** In marital terms: the cost of being right vs. the cost of sleeping alone.

III. Anecdotal Case Study: The Great Temperature War

Ankita prefers the air conditioner at 19°C. *Rohan* prefers 26°C and moral superiority.

They begin discussions in good faith. She argues from comfort; he argues from "energy efficiency." By 2 a.m., they're on opposite ends of the bed, wrapped in blankets of passive aggression.

Eventually, they arrive at a "win-win" — 22.5°C — which pleases no one but restores the illusion of rationality.

The outcome, while inefficient, is sustainable — a **Nash equilibrium** achieved through mutual fatigue.

IV. The Behavioral Dynamics

Marriage negotiations, much like corporate ones, are driven less by logic than by ego management.

Cognitive distortions at play include:

- **Anchoring Bias:** The first complaint sets the tone ("You *always* leave the cap off").
- **Loss Aversion:** The fear of giving in outweighs the joy of resolution.
- **Framing Effect:** "You never listen" sounds worse than "I feel unheard."
- **Escalation of Commitment:** Continuing an argument you've already stopped believing in.

The emotional economy of marriage thrives not on efficiency, but on **periodic recalibration.** Each conflict is an audit, not a failure.

V. Archetypes of Marital Negotiators

Archetype	Negotiation Style	Strength	Weakness
The Diplomat	Seeks harmony	Reads the room	Avoids resolution
The Litigator	Wins arguments	Precise memory	Loses affection
The Economist	Weighs trade-offs	Rational	Unbearably so
The Historian	Recalls every prior offense	Detail-oriented	Time-consuming
The Stoic	Withdraws from battle	De-escalates	Emotionally unavailable

❑ *Margin note:* "Every marriage has two lawyers — one arguing the case, and the other deciding when to settle."

VI. The Strategic Framework: BATNA and Reversion

The key to successful negotiation lies in understanding your **BATNA** — your fallback position if no agreement is reached.

In geopolitics, it's sanctions. In business, it's walking away. In marriage, it's the **couch.**

The couch is both symbol and sanction — the physical manifestation of stalemate. Sleeping on it represents a temporary reversion to independent operations.

Paradoxically, the couch stabilizes the system. It creates emotional cooling-off periods and enforces strategic reflection. It's marital arbitration, padded and upholstered.

VII. Anecdote Two: The Dishwasher Treaty

Meera and *Vikram* fought weekly over who loaded the dishwasher incorrectly. After six months of escalating tension and several failed "frameworks," they reached a revolutionary solution:

Whoever cooks doesn't clean. Whoever cleans gets playlist control.

The system worked. Not because it was fair, but because it was *repeatable.*

Their friends called it "marriage goals." Economists would call it **institutionalized quid pro quo.**

VIII. The Corporate Parallel

Marriage resembles long-term partnerships between firms with overlapping but non-identical goals. There are shared resources, differing incentives, and the occasional existential audit.

Corporations draft shareholder agreements; couples draft emotional constitutions — unspoken clauses like:

- "You handle relatives, I handle finances."
- "You decide vacations, I decide décor."
- "We both pretend not to remember that fight from 2021."

In business, alignment is sustained through quarterly reviews. In marriage, it's sustained through breakfast negotiations and joint Netflix sessions.

IX. The Existential Undercurrent

The purpose of negotiation isn't victory — it's coexistence. Every argument, no matter how small, asks a deeper question:

"Do you still see me?"

And every resolution, no matter how messy, whispers back:

"Yes, but please pass the salt."

Marriage is less a static deal than a living, breathing treaty — constantly amended, occasionally violated, yet rarely abandoned. The longer it lasts, the more you realize: equilibrium is not peace; it's rhythm.

X. The Moral (Clause 10: General Understanding)

The secret of lasting marriage lies in strategic surrender — knowing which battles to win, and which to frame as "learning opportunities."

Moral: In love as in business, the strongest negotiators know when compromise is the ultimate leverage.

"Marital Governance Index, 2025"

Institute for Domestic Economics reports: – 82 % of couples claim to have "healthy communication." – 57 % admit that "healthy communication" involves strategic silence. – 31 % say the couch has "played a role" in conflict resolution. Behavioral economists define marriage as **a dynamic contract with perpetual renegotiation and occasional furniture displacement.**

Epilogue Fragment: The Peace Dividend

It's midnight. The argument has wound down. One of you sighs. The other softens.

You both know no one won — and that's exactly why it worked. The thermostat is still wrong, but the silence is warm.

And in the soft glow of mutual concession, you realize: Love, at scale, is governance.

CHAPTER XXIX

EMOTIONAL LABOR AND THE HIDDEN COSTS OF SYNERGY

Or: Unseen effort and value extraction.

I. The Situation

It's 8:07 p.m. on a Tuesday. The dishwasher hums, the inbox pings, and one partner is staring absently at the wall.

The other, sensing *vibe turbulence*, asks,

"Are you okay?"

The answer — "I'm fine" — is a lie, of course. The correct interpretation is: "I am exhausted from managing everyone's emotions, including yours."

This, dear reader, is **emotional labor** — the invisible glue binding the illusion of domestic and relational efficiency.

In every household, one partner inevitably becomes the **Chief Emotional Officer (CEO)** — responsible for morale, memory, and maintaining the illusion that things are under control.

II. The Model: The Emotional Economy

Emotional labor, like organizational maintenance, operates through **asymmetric visibility**: the more seamlessly it's done, the less it's noticed.

Function	Description	Visibility	Example
Emotional Regulation	Managing tone, moods, and reactions	Low	"It's okay, we'll figure it out."
Relationship Forecasting	Anticipating conflict, preemptive apologies	Very Low	"Let's not bring this up right now."
Moral Accounting	Tracking favors, remembering birthdays	Medium	"You forgot our anniversary again."
Social Diplomacy	Managing in-laws, group chats, awkward friends	Negative	"I'll handle it."

Economists would describe this as **emotional externalities** — unpaid costs absorbed by one party for collective stability. Therapists call it *"carrying the emotional spreadsheet."*

III. Anecdotal Case Study: The Invisible COO

Priya and *Aditya* both worked full-time. He managed "big things" — finances, investments, long-term planning. She managed "everything else" — meals, moods, memories, logistics, apologies.

When asked if labor was equally divided, Aditya said,

"Of course! I cook on Sundays."

Priya smiled, because that was easier than auditing the spreadsheet.

In project management terms, she was performing **continuous integration** — seamlessly merging emotional code while he ran quarterly strategy reviews.

Her burnout was not sudden; it was accrued — the silent depreciation of an unaccounted asset.

IV. The Behavioral Dynamics

Why does emotional labor remain invisible? Because it's **measured by absence** — you only notice it when it stops.

Psychological biases sustaining this imbalance include:

- **The Effort Invisibility Trap:** Familiar labor fades into background noise.
- **The Competence Paradox:** The more capable the emotional laborer, the more invisible the work.
- **The Empathy Tax:** Those who care more, do more, and then get accused of "overreacting."
- **The Optimization Fallacy:** The belief that emotions can be systematized through "communication frameworks."

It's a quiet irony: the people who manage everyone's feelings are often accused of being "too emotional."

V. Archetypes of Emotional Laborers

Archetype	Primary Function	Typical Burnout Symptom
The Empath	Absorbs moods	Emotional fatigue
The Organizer	Manages schedules and crises	Sleep deprivation
The Buffer	Smooths over tension	Quiet resentment

Archetype	Primary Function	Typical Burnout Symptom
The Fixer	Solves problems unasked	Chronic disappointment
The Martyr	Performs visible exhaustion	Occasional weaponized sighs

🗨 *Margin note:* "In every relationship, one person keeps the peace. The other benefits from stable governance."

VI. The Strategic Framework: Hidden Synergy Costs

In corporate strategy, **synergy** refers to the added value created by collaboration — but it also hides integration costs. In relationships, these integration costs are emotional.

Every joint decision — from vacation plans to parenting — carries transaction costs: time, empathy, patience. If one partner consistently pays more of these, the system becomes unsustainable.

The solution isn't symmetry — it's **rotation of roles.** Take turns being the emotionally responsible adult. True equality isn't division of labor; it's division of *effort consciousness.*

VII. Anecdote Two: The Calendar of Compassion

Manish prided himself on being a supportive husband. When his wife *Leena* broke down from exhaustion one evening, he said gently,

"Why didn't you just tell me you were overwhelmed?"

Leena, staring at the dinner she'd just cooked after her 10-hour shift, replied,

"Because then I'd have to manage your guilt too."

That line, if printed in Harvard Business Review, would end a thousand panel discussions on "work-life balance."

What Manish missed was that **asking for help is itself labor** when help requires instruction.

VIII. The Corporate Parallel

Emotional labor in relationships mirrors **culture work** in organizations. A handful of people (often women, often unacknowledged) sustain morale, mediate conflicts, and remember birthdays — without ever getting formal credit.

Executives call it "team spirit." HR calls it "employee engagement." It's actually **uncompensated affective maintenance.**

The firm thrives, just as the marriage does, because someone quietly performs unpaid optimism.

IX. The Existential Undercurrent

To love is to labor, yes — but when that labor becomes one-sided, it transforms into servitude dressed as sensitivity.

The tragedy isn't that emotional labor exists. It's that it's mistaken for *personality.*

We reward composure, not balance. We praise patience but rarely reciprocate it. And somewhere in this quiet asymmetry, affection turns administrative.

Perhaps love's truest evolution lies in shared exhaustion — the ability to say,

"I see how hard you're holding this together. Let me hold it for a while."

X. The Moral (Footnote to an Invisible Ledger)

Relationships don't fail because people stop loving — they fail because one person keeps managing.

Moral: True partnership begins the day emotional labor becomes a *shared service*, not a hidden cost center.

"Domestic Synergy Index, 2025"

Institute for Relational Economics reports: – 71 % of couples say they have "equal partnerships." – 64 % of women and 18 % of men disagree with that statement. – 49 % of respondents report "being the emotional default." Behavioral economists define emotional labor as **a recurring cost with no depreciation schedule and infinite renewal expectations.**

Epilogue Fragment: The Invisible Dividend

It's 11:43 p.m. You send a text reminder to your partner about their mother's birthday tomorrow. You fold the laundry you didn't wear. You sigh — softly, but with purpose.

Somewhere deep down, you know this: Love's truest measure isn't in grand gestures, but in who remembers what keeps the day from collapsing.

You turn off the lights and whisper into the darkness,

"Tomorrow, I'll renegotiate."

CHAPTER XXX

BREAKUPS AS STRATEGIC DIVESTMENTS

> *Or: Loss minimization and brand repositioning.*

I. The Situation

It starts, as most endings do, with the sound of gentle ambiguity.

"We need to talk." "It's not you, it's timing." "I just need space."

Space, of course, is corporate for *we're downsizing.*

Every breakup, whether abrupt or gradual, is a divestment — a restructuring of emotional assets that once promised exponential returns. The relationship, once a bullish investment in shared futures, is now a declining stock in denial.

And so begins the most painful stage of portfolio management: **strategic withdrawal.**

II. The Model: The Emotional Divestment Cycle

Phase	Business Equivalent	Description	Typical Behavior
Due Diligence	Performance Review	Subtle audit of partner's ROI	"Are we okay?" texts

Phase	Business Equivalent	Description	Typical Behavior
Warning Signals	Market Correction	Declining affection, increased distraction	"I've just been busy."
Announcement	Press Release	Polite exit narrative	"You deserve better."
Wind-Down	Asset Liquidation	Returning gifts, deleting photos	Strategic denial
Repositioning	Rebranding	"I'm focusing on myself."	New haircut, new bio

Each breakup moves through the same **grief funnel**, from disbelief to detachment to Instagram wisdom. What distinguishes survivors from serial mourners is *change management.*

III. Anecdotal Case Study: The Clean Exit Myth

Arjun and *Maya* dated for two years — a well-diversified emotional portfolio. When the end came, they agreed to "remain friends," a phrase as credible as "synergy through downsizing."

Three months later, they were still "catching up" weekly, maintaining *legacy operations* long after dissolution. The breakup, though publicly clean, was privately messy — proof that **emotional assets rarely liquidate without residual interest.**

It finally ended when Maya found someone new. Arjun congratulated her, then muted her stories. Thus concluded the divestment — not with a signature, but a scroll.

IV. The Behavioral Dynamics

Breaking up is less about emotion than *identity demerger.* Two entities who once shared resources must now disentangle brand narratives, supply chains, and joint intellectual property (a.k.a. inside jokes).

Key psychological biases that complicate exits:

- **Sunk Cost Fallacy:** "We've been together so long — it can't end now."
- **Endowment Effect:** Overvaluing what you already own (or used to).
- **Confirmation Bias:** Interpreting nostalgia as a signal for revival.
- **Loss Aversion:** Preferring misery to uncertainty.

We call it "holding on," but it's really just *refusing to take the write-off.*

V. Archetypes of Post-Breakup Strategists

Archetype	Exit Strategy	Market Outcome
The Clean Cutter	Deletes everything instantly	Appears stoic, cries at 3 a.m.
The Archivist	Keeps all memories "for closure"	Lives in emotional archives
The Serial Rebounder	Reinvests immediately	Diversifies losses poorly

Archetype	Exit Strategy	Market Outcome
The Sabbatical Taker	Goes off-grid, journals, returns wiser	High growth potential
The Brand Rebuilder	Posts motivational quotes	Monetizes healing

🗨 *Margin note:* "Some people move on. Others conduct quarterly reviews with ghosts."

VI. The Strategic Framework: Exit Planning and Value Preservation

Smart companies don't divest in panic — they plan exits to protect brand equity. The same principle applies to breakups: you must separate *the product (you)* from *the partnership (us).*

1. **Announce Gradually:** Sudden exits cause market shock.
2. **Communicate Transparently:** Ambiguity fuels rumors and rebound volatility.
3. **Preserve Reputation:** No post-breakup press leaks (subtweets, playlists, cryptic captions).
4. **Audit Emotional Assets:** Reclaim hobbies, friendships, and self-worth.
5. **Reinvest in R&D:** Rediscover who you are without shared branding.

The goal isn't to win the breakup — it's to **survive the rebrand without losing authenticity.**

VII. Anecdote Two: The Soft Launch of Solitude

Leela's breakup didn't involve yelling, tears, or betrayal. It was a polite memo titled *"I think we've become different people."*

In the weeks that followed, she stopped sharing memes, then stopped checking his last seen. Her friends called it "graceful." She called it "numb."

It wasn't until she repotted her shared plants alone that she realized the breakup had finally gone live.

Her healing wasn't a sprint — it was a **slow operational shutdown**. No grand closure, just quiet offboarding.

VIII. The Corporate Parallel

In business, divestments are essential for agility — shedding underperforming units to reallocate focus. Yet they're never clean. There are legacy systems, intertwined processes, brand dependencies.

Just like in love.

Companies reissue statements. Lovers reframe narratives. Both claim, *"We're still on good terms."* Both secretly hope the other side underperforms post-split.

The best-managed exits — like the best breakups — are those where both parties grow, but neither gloats.

IX. The Existential Undercurrent

To end a relationship is to face the quiet collapse of a shared story. You are no longer a "we," but a "me with memories." The hardest part isn't loss — it's *repositioning identity after merger failure.*

And yet, endings are strangely generative. They force introspection, create space, and remind us that not every investment was meant for lifetime holding.

Sometimes you divest not because it failed — but because its purpose was fulfilled. A good breakup, like a good strategy, is a lesson in graceful retreat.

X. The Moral (Final Audit)

Love and business share the same unspoken rule: exit cleanly, account honestly, and don't badmouth your ex to potential partners.

Moral: Every ending is an IPO of solitude — trade wisely.

"The Heartbreak Index, 2025"

Institute for Relational Economics reports: – 63 % of people report "feeling like a failure" post-breakup. – 41 % experience "post-divestment rebranding" via haircuts or travel. – 12 % "reacquire" their ex within six months. Behavioral economists define heartbreak as **emotional depreciation misattributed to market volatility.**

Epilogue Fragment: The Rebrand

You change your display picture. You rearrange your playlist. You start sleeping diagonally again.

At first it feels wrong — too much space, too little noise. But gradually, you realize: this is not emptiness; it's liquidity.

Some assets aren't meant to be held. They're meant to teach you valuation.

ARC VI: FROM THE STREET TO THE C-SUITE

EVERYDAY WISDOM FOR CORPORATE MINDS

CHAPTER XXXI

LAUNDRY AS PROCESS OPTIMIZATION

Or: Batch processing and inventory control.

I. The Situation

Laundry, like most modern operations, begins with denial.

You see the growing pile. You pretend it's still within "manageable backlog." You start calculating load economics — "if I wait two more days, I can wash it all at once and *save water*."

This, of course, is a lie. By the time you act, the hamper has achieved critical mass and a faint odor of deferred responsibility.

And yet, every week, we repeat the cycle — a ritual of inefficiency disguised as domestic virtue.

II. The Model: The Laundry Supply Chain

Corporate supply chains involve procurement, production, quality control, and distribution. Laundry, tragically, mirrors this almost perfectly:

Stage	Equivalent	Description	Strategic Failure
Procurement	Dirty Clothes Collection	The "inflow" problem — underreported inventory	Delays due to denial
Processing	Washing Cycle	The operational bottleneck	Overloaded machines (a.k.a. scope creep)
Quality Assurance	Folding & Sorting	Inspection & rework	"I'll do it later" fallacy
Distribution	Putting Away	Final-mile delivery	Abandonment at 95% completion

The average human spends 8 years of life in some stage of this process. That's an entire MBA in *operational inefficiency.*

If Toyota had designed our homes, the washing machine would email us when idle time exceeded acceptable throughput. Instead, we rely on *gut feel and guilt.*

III. Anecdotal Case Study: The Great Sock Disappearance

Case Reference No. LDRY-0421

Subject: *Neha, 34, working professional, two children, one washing machine with dreams beyond its pay grade.*

Problem: Chronic sock attrition — one per load.

Hypothesis: Systemic inefficiency or existential rebellion?

Upon investigation, the missing socks were not "lost." They were absorbed into the *entropy cost* of the process — the tax life imposes on anyone who believes in symmetry.

Economists would call it **inventory shrinkage.** Philosophers would call it **the acceptance of imperfection.** Parents simply buy more socks.

IV. Behavioral Insights

Laundry exposes every behavioral bias known to humankind:

- **Procrastination Bias:** The belief that tomorrow's version of you will be more industrious and less resentful.
- **Batching Fallacy:** Assuming bigger loads equal higher efficiency, ignoring the law of diminishing returns (and detergent).
- **Completion Illusion:** Feeling productive after starting the cycle, even if you abandon folding.
- **Delegation Fantasy:** Believing "someone else" in the household will finish it.

Laundry isn't just a task — it's a weekly reminder of our inability to manage time, inventory, and hope simultaneously.

V. Archetypes of the Domestic Operator

Archetype	Approach	Outcome
The Maximalist	Waits till no clean clothes remain	Lives perpetually at the edge of chaos
The Micro-Manager	Washes daily, folds hourly	Mistakes motion for efficiency
The Innovator	Outsources to service apps	Learns about quality control the hard way
The Philosopher	Accepts wrinkles as a metaphor	Sleeps peacefully, slightly musty

Archetype	Approach	Outcome
The Analyst	Tracks detergent usage and fabric wear	Loses friends but gains graphs

🗨 *Margin note:* "Every family has one person who folds like a consultant — and another who folds like an artist."

VI. The Strategic Framework: Lean Laundry Management

Applying **Lean principles** to domestic operations yields surprising parallels:

1. **Eliminate Waste (Muda):** Stop re-washing clothes you forgot in the machine overnight.
2. **Optimize Flow:** Designate a single "laundry day" — not because it's efficient, but because it limits guilt to one 24-hour period.
3. **Pull, Don't Push:** Wash only when inventory (hamper) demand triggers the process — not when anxiety does.
4. **Continuous Improvement (Kaizen):** Experiment with folding techniques until one doesn't spark existential dread.

By implementing these, you too can transform laundry from a chore into a **process improvement initiative with questionable ROI.**

VII. Anecdote Two: The White Shirt Crisis

Ravi once attempted to wash his office whites with his gym clothes — a cross-functional synergy project gone wrong.

The result? Every shirt turned a faint shade of despair.

He called it "off-white." His boss called it "unemployable."

From that day forward, Ravi separated loads with religious zeal — an act of operational discipline that saved his wardrobe, if not his dignity.

Moral of the case: **Segregation is not just ethical — it's logistical.**

VIII. The Corporate Parallel

Every office has its version of the laundry pile — neglected projects, outdated systems, lingering "action items" no one wants to claim.

Quarterly reviews, like spin cycles, promise cleansing but merely redistribute dirt. Meetings act as detergent: foamy, fragrant, and only marginally effective.

True leaders understand that **process optimization begins not with doing more, but with stopping what doesn't work.** Even a CEO is just a glorified laundry sorter — deciding what gets cleaned, what gets folded, and what quietly disappears.

IX. The Existential Undercurrent

There's something deeply human in laundry's futility. No matter how efficient you become, the pile returns — entropy disguised as cotton.

And yet, it comforts us. Each cycle, though repetitive, feels like redemption — proof that order, however temporary, can be restored.

Perhaps that's why people meditate while ironing. It's not about creases. It's about control — the illusion that we can press chaos into form.

X. The Moral (Washed, Rinsed, Repeated)

Efficiency isn't about doing laundry faster — it's about doing it with acceptance. Because in the end, we aren't optimizing garments; we're optimizing surrender.

Moral: Process mastery begins when you stop expecting the pile to end.

"Domestic Efficiency Index, 2025"

Institute for Applied Household Strategy reports: – 72 % of people claim to have a "system." – 63 % of those systems involve "panic folding." – 14 % say laundry "teaches discipline." Behavioral economists define laundry as **a recurring process with no terminal value but high symbolic yield.**

Epilogue Fragment: The Folded Life

You fold a shirt. You stack it neatly. You feel momentarily accomplished. Then you glance at the next pile, and realize: the cycle never ends.

Still, you smile. Because in that Sisyphean spin of cloth and care, you glimpse something sacred — a tiny act of order in a universe that never stays clean for long.

CHAPTER XXXII

PARENTING AS TALENT DEVELOPMENT

> *Or: Feedback loops, psychological safety, and succession planning.*

I. The Situation

Every new parent begins like a first-time CEO: overconfident, underqualified, and convinced they'll "do things differently."

They read articles about growth mindsets, listen to parenting podcasts, and declare noble mission statements like:

"We won't bribe our child with candy."

Two years later, they're whispering,

"If you brush your teeth, you get chocolate."

And thus, like every management philosophy before it, *idealism yields to practicality.*

II. The Model: The Family as an Organization

Every household, whether chaotic or calm, operates like a miniature corporation — complete with departments, workflows, and performance reviews that no one remembers agreeing to.

Department	Function	Typical Leadership Failure
HR	Emotional regulation, conflict resolution	Over-reliance on hugs as policy
Operations	Meals, routines, logistics	Chronic scope creep (bedtime delayed by 47 minutes)
Finance	Allowance management	Budget leakages: "ice cream emergencies"
Training	Skill development, manners	Misaligned KPIs between parents
Audit	Grandparents	Interference disguised as wisdom

Parenting, like management, requires balancing **nurture and structure** — too much freedom breeds chaos; too much control breeds rebellion. The challenge is to produce a self-sustaining successor before your own operational capacity collapses.

III. Anecdotal Case Study: The Bedtime Resistance Movement

Subject: Ananya, 6; Parents: exhausted; Objective: sleep before 9:30 p.m.

Each night, the project followed a predictable pattern:

- Stage 1: Negotiation ("One more story?")
- Stage 2: Deflection ("But I'm not sleepy.")
- Stage 3: Resistance ("I will *never* sleep again.")
- Stage 4: Attrition ("Okay fine, but I want water.")

- Stage 5: Compliance ("Can you lie down with me?")

In corporate terms, this was a **protracted merger negotiation**, with shifting deadlines and asymmetric power.

The parents' mistake? Treating bedtime as a *command*, not a *process*. Smart leaders know: compliance without buy-in is temporary.

So they introduced incentives — stars, stickers, and bedtime stories of heroic compliance. By week three, the system stabilized — until, of course, she realized *she could renegotiate for longer stories.*

This is how **feedback loops** evolve into *mutually assured exhaustion.*

IV. The Behavioral Dynamics

Parenting, much like leadership, is 20 % instruction and 80 % emotional improvisation.

Key behavioral insights:

- **The Illusion of Control:** Believing you can "mold" personality instead of merely influencing environment.
- **Projection Bias:** Expecting your child to mirror your ambitions, fears, or caffeine preferences.
- **The Halo Effect:** Overrating intelligence because they used a big word once ("existential").
- **Survivorship Bias:** Forgetting that your own parents didn't have parenting books and you still survived (mostly).

The best parents — and the best managers — learn to guide, not dictate. The worst assume authority equals wisdom.

V. Archetypes of Parental Leadership

Archetype	Leadership Style	Outcome
The Visionary	"Dream big!"	Inspires imagination, forgets breakfast
The Micro-Manager	"Do it exactly like this."	Produces obedient employees, not thinkers
The Enabler	"As long as you're happy."	Encourages creativity, erodes boundaries
The Bureaucrat	"Because I said so."	Efficient, resented
The Agile Coach	"Let's reflect on what went wrong."	Exhausted but emotionally evolved

🗨 *Margin note:* "A child's first boss is their parent — and most resign emotionally before adolescence."

VI. The Strategic Framework: Feedback Loops and Psychological Safety

In business, **feedback loops** are designed to refine performance. In parenting, they're designed to prevent chaos.

Good feedback has three qualities: timely, specific, and kind. Which is exactly why it fails at home — because we usually deliver it while shouting over spilled milk.

Creating **psychological safety** for children mirrors creating it in teams:

- Allow mistakes without humiliation.
- Model accountability ("I was wrong to yell.").
- Encourage curiosity, not compliance.
- Use humor as lubrication for correction.

Children — like employees — thrive not under fear, but under predictable compassion.

VII. Anecdote Two: The Succession Planning Fiasco

Rajesh prided himself on being "hands-on." When his teenage son *Aarav* forgot to submit an assignment, Rajesh stayed up until 1 a.m. finishing it himself.

He considered it love. Aarav considered it *outsourcing*.

Years later, Rajesh would lament that his son "lacks ownership." But the truth was simpler: **he'd never been allowed to fail.**

Succession planning isn't about ensuring continuity — it's about letting go. Leaders who can't delegate end up raising dependents, not successors.

VIII. The Corporate Parallel

Corporations that smother talent with control breed mediocrity. Families that do the same breed adults who need HR policies to manage emotions.

The most successful organizations — and households — are those that practice **autonomy with accountability.**

- Google gives engineers 20 % time for personal projects.
- Great parents give kids 20 % time to make ridiculous messes.

Both approaches produce innovation — and occasional disasters.

IX. The Existential Undercurrent

Parenting isn't a legacy project; it's a long, slow relinquishment of control. You begin as the architect, become the advisor, and end as a silent investor.

The goal isn't to create a "better version" of yourself — it's to raise someone capable of becoming *someone else entirely.*

And yet, like every founder watching a startup grow beyond them, there's bittersweet pride in realizing: they don't need you as much anymore.

That's not failure — that's succession.

X. The Moral (Filed Under: "Ongoing Project")

The best managers and parents share one rare quality: they know when to stop managing.

Moral: True leadership isn't about shaping the next generation — it's about equipping them to ignore your advice intelligently.

"Household Leadership Index, 2025"

Institute for Domestic Development Studies reports: – 68 % of parents describe themselves as "supportive." – 54 % of children describe that support as "micromanagement." – 81 % of all conflicts originate from "tone of voice." Behavioral economists define parenting as **a multi-decade mentorship program with no graduation ceremony and infinite feedback loops.**

Epilogue Fragment: The Gentle Offboarding

You watch your child tie their shoes without help. You feel the strange ache of redundancy — part pride, part panic.

They smile at you — impatient, independent. You remember every night you thought you'd fail them. Turns out, that fear *was* the training.

And so you let go, just a little. Because leadership, like love, ends not with authority — but with trust.

CHAPTER XXXIII

TRAFFIC JAMS AND ORGANIZATIONAL BUREAUCRACY

Or: Congestion management and process simplification.

I. The Situation

You're on your way to work. Theoretically. You left early, took the "shorter route," and now find yourself staring at the same billboard for fifteen minutes — the one advertising productivity apps that promise to "save time."

You switch lanes three times. None helps. Someone cuts you off. Someone else honks at air. You glance at the navigation app: *"5 minutes delay ahead."* It's been saying that for 25 minutes.

Congratulations — you are living in a case study of **organizational inefficiency**, where every driver believes they're the exception, and thus collectively prove they're not.

II. The Model: The Congestion Curve

In urban traffic — as in corporate bureaucracy — the system fails not because people don't move, but because **everyone moves at once.**

System Variable	Traffic Equivalent	Corporate Parallel	Failure Mode
Volume	Number of vehicles	Number of stakeholders	Overload
Flow Rate	Lane capacity	Approval bandwidth	Bottleneck
Signaling	Traffic lights	Communication channels	Delay and miscoordination
Incentive Structure	"I'll reach faster"	"I'll just CC everyone"	Reinforced inefficiency
Governance	Traffic cops	Middle management	Selective enforcement

Economists call it the **Braess Paradox** — the phenomenon where adding more lanes actually worsens traffic because everyone optimizes for themselves. In organizations, this is known as *"creating another team to fix coordination."*

III. Anecdotal Case Study: The Shortcut Fallacy

Case Reference: Commuter 47B, a.k.a. Rakesh, 39, believer in "better routes."

Every morning, Rakesh takes a new "shortcut" to avoid congestion. Every morning, he ends up 10 minutes later than before.

The pattern persists because he assumes information asymmetry — that he alone has discovered the secret route. Of course, everyone else on the road has read the same blog, watched the same video, and had the same idea.

Thus is born the great paradox of optimization: **collective intelligence cancels itself.**

This same principle fuels bureaucratic gridlock — every department "finding a better process," thereby spawning new forms to fill and new meetings to host.

Efficiency, at scale, becomes its own bottleneck.

IV. The Behavioral Dynamics

Traffic and bureaucracy are both psychological ecosystems of **learned helplessness.** Nobody believes the system works, but everyone fears deviating from it.

Some behavioral biases in play:

- **Optimism Bias:** "It won't be bad today."
- **Control Illusion:** "If I honk, the cars will move."
- **Social Proof:** "Everyone else is switching lanes."
- **Planning Fallacy:** "I'll leave five minutes early and it'll all be fine."
- **Moral Licensing:** "I can break this rule because I've suffered enough already."

The truth is, whether you're in traffic or in an org chart, motion is often mistaken for progress. You *feel* productive while honking — just as you *feel* useful replying "Noted."

V. Archetypes of the Congested Mind

Archetype	Traffic Behavior	Organizational Behavior	Common Outcome
The Lane Hopper	Constantly switches to faster lanes	Job-hops	Perpetual dissatisfaction
The Horn Activist	Honks to assert relevance	Sends "gentle reminders"	Alienates peers

Archetype	Traffic Behavior	Organizational Behavior	Common Outcome
The Philosopher	Accepts fate, listens to podcasts	Practices corporate stoicism	Achieves calm, not promotion
The Influencer	Films chaos for social commentary	Creates "culture decks"	Viral fame, zero impact
The Bureaucrat	Obeys every sign religiously	Follows SOP to absurdity	Promoted to traffic management

🗨 *Margin note:* "In both traffic and offices, the people who get ahead are rarely the ones following the rules — but always the ones pretending to."

VI. The Strategic Framework: Congestion Management 101

1. **Reduce Decision Points:** The more intersections (or approvals), the slower the flow. Simplify pathways — fewer emails, fewer detours.
2. **Introduce Synchronized Signals:** Coordination beats autonomy in high-density systems. Align team timelines like traffic lights — green means go, not "go and we'll discuss next week."
3. **Implement Toll Gates:** Create accountability thresholds — if you're blocking the lane, you pay (metaphorically, or ideally, actually).
4. **Encourage Off-Peak Behavior:** Incentivize asynchronous work — let people move at different times, not all at once.
5. **Monitor Throughput, Not Appearances:** Cars honking louder aren't faster. Employees sending more emails aren't more efficient.

When properly applied, these principles convert chaos into flow — or at least reduce the honking.

VII. Anecdote Two: The Roundabout of Doom

At a particularly famous intersection, five roads meet and no one yields. Each driver believes in fairness — *but only after their turn.*

A man in a small hatchback, tired of waiting, enters the roundabout halfway through a truck's turn. A cacophony ensues. Three near-misses, one stalled vehicle, and twelve angry hand gestures later, everyone eventually clears out.

Total time lost: 18 minutes. Total lesson learned: zero.

This is exactly how internal corporate meetings function — a flurry of inputs, nobody listening, everyone eventually leaving convinced they "handled it well."

VIII. The Corporate Parallel

Traffic is bureaucracy with wheels. Both systems exist to manage complexity — and both collapse under the weight of their own rules.

The corporate parking lot is often more efficient than its decision-making hierarchy. Why? Because **parking has clear rules, limited stakeholders, and visible consequences.**

Imagine if organizations adopted the same clarity:

- "You can't park here" = "You can't add this approval layer."
- "Tow zone" = "CC limit exceeded."
- "No entry" = "That project was killed last quarter."

The best managers act like skilled traffic cops — not by shouting louder, but by simplifying flow.

IX. The Existential Undercurrent

Every jam, literal or metaphorical, teaches us the same lesson: *most blockages are self-inflicted.* We build complexity to prove control, and end up controlled by it.

The miracle isn't that systems move slowly — it's that they move at all.

Perhaps this is why the calmest people in traffic are bus drivers — they've accepted that frustration doesn't change velocity.

Likewise, in bureaucracies, the true wisdom lies not in acceleration, but in acceptance — steering patiently through chaos with the quiet knowledge that all roads eventually clear.

X. The Moral (Filed Under: "Process Overload")

Whether on asphalt or in admin, the secret to flow is subtraction, not addition.

Moral: Progress begins the moment you stop trying to overtake everything ahead of you — including yourself.

"Congestion Efficiency Index, 2025"

Institute for Systemic Patience reports: – 79 % of professionals describe their workplace as "traffic-like." – 58 % believe "meetings could be emails." – 24 % of respondents honk at their screens. Behavioral economists define bureaucracy as **traffic with paperwork and longer wait times.**

Epilogue Fragment: The Quiet Lane

It's late. The road is empty. You glide home, smooth, steady, unhurried.

For a fleeting moment, you realize: The world isn't slow — *you were just rushing through it.*

The brake pedal, it turns out, was always a form of enlightenment.

CHAPTER XXXIV

STREET VENDOR STRATEGY LESSONS

Or: Dynamic pricing, customer intimacy, and adaptability.

I. The Situation

It's 8:45 a.m. Outside your office, a chai-wala is already running a high-velocity operation — two stoves, eight glasses, one bucket of optimism. His clientele includes sleep-deprived interns, philosophical security guards, and one VP who insists on "no sugar" but drinks two cups anyway.

By 10 a.m., he's pivoted to *samosas.* By noon, he's out of stock. You, meanwhile, are still waiting for procurement to approve coffee filters.

Somewhere between his battered kettle and your Excel sheets lies the fundamental truth of capitalism: **agility beats approval.**

II. The Model: The Street as a Business School

Domain	Street Vendor Application	Corporate Parallel	Key Advantage
Market Research	Observes footfall, adjusts menu daily	Data analytics dashboards	Instant feedback

Domain	Street Vendor Application	Corporate Parallel	Key Advantage
Dynamic Pricing	"Ten rupees in rain, eight in sunlight"	Surge pricing	No committee approval
Customer Intimacy	Remembers everyone's order	CRM software	Emotional stickiness
Product Innovation	Adds ginger when bored	R&D department	Zero bureaucracy
Working Capital	Cash drawer + gut feeling	Treasury division	Faster liquidity

Street entrepreneurs run on *live data,* not quarterly reports. Their P&L fits in a pocket; their KPI is smiles per cup.

III. Anecdotal Case Study: The Rain Surge

One July morning, *Farida*, a tea-vendor near Churchgate, noticed officegoers rushing in soaked, craving warmth. She raised her tea price from ₹8 to ₹12 — and sold out faster.

When asked why, she said,

"When it rains, people remember how much they need me."

Uber calls this **surge pricing.** Economists call it **inelastic demand.** Farida calls it **common sense.**

Her profit doubled that week — proof that *timing, not technology,* drives margins.

IV. The Behavioral Economics of the Street

Street vendors, consciously or not, master the behavioral playbook:

- **Anchoring:** "Normal chai ₹10" — followed by "Special Masala ₹15." Most buy the latter.
- **Loss Aversion:** "Last samosa left!" triggers existential panic.
- **Social Proof:** A small queue signals quality; people join without tasting.
- **Reciprocity:** "Extra biscuit for you, sir." Instant loyalty.
- **Endowment Effect:** Regulars defend their vendor like shareholders.

Where MBAs use frameworks, vendors use *human weather radar.*

V. Archetypes of Street Strategists

Archetype	Strength	Strategic Risk
The Charm Merchant	Builds loyalty through jokes and gossip	Oversharing = operational delay
The Price Ninja	Constantly tweaks rates	Customer confusion
The Minimalist	One product, flawless consistency	Vulnerable to trend shocks
The Diversifier	Expands menu weekly	Inventory entropy
The Visionary	Dreams of a franchise	Forgets to restock change

🗨 *Margin note:* "Every vendor is a micro-entrepreneur with a micro-MBA earned in sweat, not slides."

VI. The Strategic Framework: Adapt or Evaporate

1. **Dynamic Pricing as Empathy:** Pricing isn't greed — it's a barometer of urgency. In the heat, cheaper drinks; in

rain, pricier warmth. Demand elasticity, measured in goosebumps.
2. **Inventory as Agility:** No vendor stocks beyond the day. Forecast = gut feeling × weather report × hope.
3. **Customer Engagement:** Names remembered, jokes exchanged — brand intimacy at zero cost.
4. **Feedback Loop:** Complaints processed instantly: "Too sweet?" → Next cup fixed. Imagine that in corporate customer service.
5. **Failure Tolerance:** Burnt batch? Discard and move on. In offices, we hold post-mortems and PowerPoints.

The street teaches: iteration > perfection.

VII. Anecdote Two: The Coconut Pivot

During lockdown, *Rafiq* sold tender coconut near a closed gym. Footfall plummeted; he considered quitting.

Then he noticed dog walkers. He added a cooler of chilled water bottles — "For you, for dog also."

Sales tripled. Within a month, he was the unofficial hydration partner of Bandra's canine community.

Strategists call this a **pivot.** Rafiq just called it "listening."

VIII. The Corporate Parallel

The street vendor's edge lies in three things corporates fear:

- **Speed:** No approvals, only decisions.
- **Visibility:** Customer feedback delivered directly to the face.
- **Humility:** Every day starts at zero.

Corporations speak of "customer obsession" while hiding behind dashboards. Vendors live it. They don't need CRM tools — they have eyes.

Perhaps the real Harvard Business School is the footpath. And its alumni don't do keynotes — they just keep the kettle boiling.

IX. The Existential Undercurrent

The street vendor is the purest expression of economic hope: no guarantees, no contracts, just trust renewed one transaction at a time.

There's something beautiful about that fragile certainty — that tomorrow, people will still need tea.

While corporations spend billions on AI forecasting, he wakes up, looks at the sky, and knows the market.

Resilience, it turns out, is not a strategy. It's a habit.

X. The Moral (Served Hot)

The next time you hand a coin to a chai-wala, remember you're funding a masterclass in strategy.

Moral: Agility isn't about being fast — it's about staying human while everything else scales.

"Footpath Economics Index, 2025"

Institute for Urban Entrepreneurship reports: – 91 % of vendors change pricing daily. – 76 % claim "weather forecast more reliable than policy." – 63 % cite customer names as key asset. Behavioral economists define street entrepreneurship as **a market with zero barriers to entry and infinite barriers to consistency.**

Epilogue Fragment: The Morning MBA

You take your first sip of chai. It's hot, sweet, exactly right.

Behind that perfect temperature lies a chain of micro decisions faster than any algorithm.

You look at the vendor, smiling, balancing a dozen orders without a spreadsheet. And you realize — strategy is not the art of thinking ahead. It's the art of staying alive while you do.

CHAPTER XXXV

THE NEIGHBORHOOD GOSSIP NETWORK

Or: Informal communication systems and shadow hierarchies.

I. The Situation

Every neighborhood has its central nervous system — not the power grid, not the internet, but the *people who know.*

You know the type: The aunty who knows who's moving, who's marrying, who's mysteriously "studying abroad." The uncle who knows the property rates, the local MLA's mood, and the exact time the water supply resumes.

They are *nodes* in a network of whispered updates, passive-aggressive insights, and unsolicited public relations.

They don't need credentials. They have credibility — the kind that comes from being *first to know.*

II. The Model: The Informal Information Economy

In formal organizations, information flows through structure. In informal systems, it flows through *trust, curiosity, and strategic tea breaks.*

Component	Neighborhood Equivalent	Corporate Parallel	Key Feature
Information Source	Aunties, shopkeepers, delivery agents	Internal memos	Low latency, high bias
Distribution Channel	Balconies, WhatsApp groups	Email threads	Viral velocity
Governance Mechanism	Social norms, fear of embarrassment	HR policy	Enforced reputationally
Reward System	Social status, entertainment	Bonuses	Immediate dopamine payoff

The neighborhood operates as a **complex adaptive system** — decentralized, resilient, and impossible to shut down.

Attempts to contain it (e.g., "Please don't tell anyone") only make it stronger.

III. Anecdotal Case Study: The Birthday Leak

In *Colony C-6*, Ritu planned a surprise 50th birthday for her husband. By evening, the entire neighborhood — including the caterer's second cousin — knew.

When she asked her friend Meenal, "Did you tell anyone?" Meenal replied, "Of course not! I only mentioned it casually to Shreya because she promised not to tell *anyone else.*"

That phrase — *"anyone else"* — is the linguistic equivalent of clicking "Reply All."

The surprise was ruined, but the event attendance tripled. Because in information economies, **secrecy is just marketing in stealth mode.**

IV. Behavioral Dynamics

The gossip network thrives on three universal drivers: **information asymmetry, boredom, and validation.**

Key psychological levers:

- **Curiosity Bias:** The brain rewards discovery, even when it's nonsense.
- **Social Proof:** "If everyone's talking about it, it must be true."
- **Moral Licensing:** "I'm not gossiping, I'm *concerned.*"
- **Status Signaling:** Being an insider equals power.
- **Narrative Bias:** Truth is less satisfying than a well-structured rumor.

Every neighborhood rumor begins as observation, evolves into insight, and matures into myth. It's the *innovation pipeline of small talk.*

V. Archetypes of the Informal Information Officer

Archetype	Operating Style	Strategic Advantage	Failure Mode
The Hub	Central collector and distributor	Network authority	Scandal fatigue
The Analyst	Verifies, interprets, cross-references	Perceived credibility	Overconfidence

Archetype	Operating Style	Strategic Advantage	Failure Mode
The Amplifier	Adds flair, context, adjectives	Virality	Exaggeration
The Ghost	Knows everything, tells nothing	Aura of mystique	Irrelevance
The Archivist	Recalls events from 1998	Contextual memory	Unwillingness to move on

🗨 *Margin note:* "In every gossip ecosystem, the truth is just the raw material for better storytelling."

VI. The Strategic Framework: Informal Communication Systems

In organizational theory, informal communication channels are often called the **grapevine.** But the neighborhood grapevine is a *Banyan tree* — roots everywhere, impossible to uproot.

Key strategic insights:

1. **Speed Trumps Accuracy:** By the time truth catches up, the story's already monetized in attention.
2. **Decentralization Ensures Survival:** When one node goes silent, others proliferate.
3. **Trust Is Currency:** People don't need facts — they need believable sources.
4. **Containment Is Futile:** The only way to manage gossip is to feed it selectively.
5. **Feedback Loops:** Gossip self-corrects through repetition — lies eventually become folklore, not scandal.

In short: **control the narrative, not the noise.**

VII. Anecdote Two: The Cooperative Coup

In a middle-class housing society, a faction of residents plotted to replace the association president — Mr. Sinha — due to his "autocratic rule over parking spaces."

The coup began as whispered discontent at the jogging track. Within a week, it had escalated into memes, petitions, and a Google Form titled *"For the Betterment of Residents (and Parking)."*

By Sunday, Sinha resigned citing "personal reasons."

No votes were cast, no meetings held — yet the transition was smooth. Harvard calls it *shadow governance.* Sociologists call it *collective whisper democracy.*

VIII. The Corporate Parallel

The gossip network is the neighborhood's **internal communications department** — minus PowerPoint, plus passion.

Organizations try to suppress gossip, not realizing it's an early-warning system. Gossip reveals what's *emotionally true* even when factually false.

In corporations:

- The hallway chat = the balcony rumor.
- The Slack DM = the kitchen whisper.
- The "informal catch-up" = the 5 p.m. chai circle.

Smart leaders tune into gossip — not to punish it, but to diagnose it. Because wherever formal channels fail, informal ones compensate.

IX. The Existential Undercurrent

Why do we gossip at all? Because gossip is storytelling with stakes. It's how we make sense of a chaotic world — by turning random events into narrative coherence.

It's also how we stay human in systems that try to make us efficient. Gossip is inefficient — gloriously so. It refuses to be optimized, monetized, or automated.

In an era of algorithms, gossip remains our last analog instinct — messy, emotional, beautifully human.

X. The Moral (Filed Under: "Classified")

Gossip isn't the enemy of truth — it's the rehearsal for it. Before history is written, it's whispered.

Moral: The most powerful networks aren't formal — they're the ones people deny exist while constantly using them.

"Neighborhood Information Efficiency Index, 2025"

Institute for Social Dynamics reports: – 83 % of households admit to "light gossip." – 97 % of those deny being the *source.* – 100 % believe "someone else spreads rumors." Behavioral economists define gossip as **a low-cost, high-velocity information exchange with unpredictable accuracy and infinite engagement.**

Epilogue Fragment: The Whisper as Infrastructure

The lights flicker, the Wi-Fi dies, but the gossip continues. It doesn't need servers, networks, or data plans — just people with time, tea, and trust.

You smile as someone tells you, "Did you hear?" Of course you did. But you'll still listen. Because in a world drowning in data, rumor is the last refuge of wonder.

CHAPTER XXXVI

THE ART OF DOING NOTHING

Or: Strategic inaction, slack time, and the wisdom of delay.

I. The Situation

You're sitting on your couch, staring at a half-finished to-do list that has begun reproducing like bacteria. Your phone buzzes with reminders: "Respond to that email," "Order groceries," "Update your LinkedIn headline to sound purposeful."

You sigh and do nothing.

Immediately, guilt arrives like a push notification from capitalism: *"You're wasting time."*

But what if you aren't? What if, in the grand chessboard of modern life, your inaction is the most efficient move — a deliberate non-move designed to let others reveal their strategy first?

As the great strategist of sofa cushions once said:

"Even a paused browser tab conserves energy."

II. The Model: The Strategic Slack Curve

Organizations (and overachievers) often confuse *utilization* with *productivity*. They believe 100% utilization equals 100% efficiency. In reality, that's how systems collapse.

Variable	Ideal Level	Overload Outcome
Resource Utilization	80–85%	Burnout / Bottleneck

Variable	Ideal Level	Overload Outcome
Decision Velocity	Moderated	Errors, rework
Meeting Density	Low	Group fatigue
Response Urgency	Contextual	Panic disguised as efficiency

This is the **Slack Time Paradox**:

The busier you are, the less time you have to think — and thus the busier you remain.

Nature knows this. Muscles grow not during strain, but during rest. So do ideas.

III. Anecdotal Case Study: The Lazy Genius

Meet *Vikram*, a mid-level manager who perfected the art of "delayed engagement." In meetings, when asked for updates, he'd smile and say, "I'm observing how the landscape evolves."

Translation: *He was waiting to see if the problem would solve itself.* And astonishingly, it often did.

By simply not reacting, Vikram became known for "strategic patience" — which is corporate-speak for "didn't panic first."

He's now a director. The hyperactive problem-solvers? Still updating PowerPoints.

IV. Behavioral Dynamics: The Myth of Motion

Our cultural wiring equates idleness with failure. But idleness, properly managed, is **latent potential.**

The key cognitive biases at play:

- **Action Bias:** The compulsion to do *something*, even when doing nothing is smarter.
- **Urgency Illusion:** The belief that fast decisions are better ones.
- **Busyness Signaling:** Performing activity to appear valuable.
- **Availability Heuristic:** Overvaluing immediate outcomes over latent ones.

Strategic stillness isn't laziness — it's the discipline to *not flinch first.* Every chess master knows the power of a long pause. Every toddler knows it too — right before throwing the plate.

V. Archetypes of Strategic Inaction

Archetype	Strength	Hidden Power	Failure Mode
The Watchful Owl	Observes before acting	Pattern recognition	Paralysis by analysis
The Tortoise	Moves slow but steady	Timing and endurance	Underestimation
The Stoic	Unmoved by chaos	Emotional resilience	Disengagement
The Opportunist	Waits for mistakes	Exploits system drift	Reputation risk
The Hermit	Retreats to think	Clarity	Isolation

🗨 *Margin note:* "Doing nothing only seems foolish until everyone else burns out doing something."

VI. The Framework: The Three Modes of Inaction

1. Tactical Delay:

Used to let information mature. Equivalent to marinating an idea before serving it. (Also known as: "Let's circle back next week.")

2. Reflective Slack:

Intentional breathing space that allows insight to surface. This is the corporate nap of the mind. Most breakthroughs are born here — usually in the shower, never in meetings.

3. Strategic Abandonment:

The boldest form of doing nothing: walking away. To realize that not every battle deserves a budget, and not every email needs a reply.

The highest level of leadership is discernment — not effort.

VII. Anecdote Two: The Great Delay Dividend

In 2020, an urban planning committee in Pune debated whether to build a costly flyover or "observe traffic for six months." They chose the latter.

Three months later, a new metro route diverted 40% of traffic. Problem solved — at zero cost.

Public outrage turned to applause. The committee was hailed for "visionary patience."

Translation: **they waited.** And sometimes, that's enough.

VIII. The Corporate Parallel

Companies love action verbs: *Launch. Scale. Transform. Optimize.* But the great ones master the silent ones: *Pause. Observe. Wait.*

- Toyota calls it **Jidoka** — stopping the line to fix problems at the source.
- Google calls it **20% time** — deliberate slack for creativity.
- Monks call it **Tuesday.**

Strategic inaction builds optionality — the capacity to act *later* with better information. The impatient organization acts first and iterates forever.

IX. The Existential Undercurrent

In truth, doing nothing terrifies us because it confronts us with ourselves. Motion distracts from meaning.

But silence — or stillness — reveals how much of our urgency is self-created theater. Maybe that's why the ancients worshipped rest days and sabbaths: not as laziness, but as rebellion against perpetual motion.

In a world that monetizes attention, stillness is the last act of freedom.

X. The Moral (Filed Under: "Zen MBA")

Doing nothing is not a pause in progress — it's progress in disguise.

Moral: The smartest strategy is sometimes to let the world move first — and then take credit for the direction it chose.

"Inactivity Productivity Index, 2025"

Institute for Cognitive Efficiency reports: – 73 % of professionals admit to solving problems "by waiting them out." – 54 % of breakthroughs occur during breaks, not brainstorms. – 91 % of Slack users wish for more slack. Behavioral economists define inaction as **the active management of entropy through selective laziness.**

Epilogue Fragment: The Still Point

The emails are sent. The meetings are over. You sit. Nothing moves.

And in that brief, unmonetized moment, the mind breathes again.

The world, it turns out, doesn't collapse when you do nothing. It just rearranges itself — quietly, efficiently, beautifully — around your stillness.

EPILOGUE: THE OPTIONAL SIX

BECAUSE NO FRAMEWORK IS COMPLETE

WITHOUT OVERFITTING

CHAPTER XXXVII

THE SELF-HELP INDUSTRIAL COMPLEX

> *Or: Monetizing mindfulness and the strategy of selling strategy.*

I. The Situation

You wake up feeling slightly inadequate. Not dramatically so — just enough to know that someone, somewhere, is monetizing your mild discontent.

Instagram suggests "5 Morning Routines of Millionaires." You scroll through them while still in bed, eating toast.

You watch a video where a man in a linen shirt tells you to *"be intentional."* You nod solemnly, right before opening five more tabs on *how to be intentional.*

And then it hits you: **You're not living a life anymore — you're beta-testing one.**

The modern self-help industry has turned introspection into infrastructure. Mindfulness is now a subscription service, and personal growth is just another KPI.

II. The Business Model of Betterment

The Self-Help Industrial Complex runs on a deceptively simple loop:

1. **Diagnose a universal emotion** (anxiety, procrastination, guilt).
2. **Rebrand it as a solvable problem.**
3. **Sell a framework, course, or journal promising measurable change.**
4. **Ensure recurrence by leaving the cure incomplete.**

It's the only business where customer retention equals continued suffering.

Product	Promise	Core Mechanic
Productivity Apps	"Be your best self."	Infinite notifications
Coaching Programs	"Unlock your potential."	Perpetual mentorship dependency
Motivational Books	"Transform your mindset."	Recycled Stoicism with emojis
Mindfulness Retreats	"Detach from materialism."	For a fee, payable in advance

Somewhere, Seneca weeps — not because we misread him, but because we turned his letters into LinkedIn carousels.

III. Anecdotal Case Study: The Subscription to Self

Neha, a mid-level executive, once bought a meditation app to "reduce stress." Three months later, she was stressed about missing her meditation streak.

She joined a "Deep Focus Bootcamp," bought a "Manifestation Journal," and signed up for a "Self-Leadership Cohort."

When asked what she'd learned, she replied:

"That I'm still not enough — but now I can describe it better."

That's when you know you've achieved *meta-mindfulness* — awareness of your awareness, monetized monthly.

IV. A Brief History of Organized Epiphany

Self-help once began nobly — as reflection, philosophy, and moral inquiry. Marcus Aurelius had his *Meditations*. The Buddha had the Bodhi tree. Thoreau had a pond.

Then capitalism discovered their unit economics.

The Stoic quote on your mug was once a hard-won realization about impermanence. Now it's a Canva template with "#GrindQuietly" in the caption.

We've replaced enlightenment with engagement. And like all engagement-driven systems, the goal isn't wisdom — it's *retention.*

V. Cross-Reference: The Strategy of Selling Strategy

If you've followed this series, you'll notice a pattern: Every domain — from kitchens to commutes — eventually industrializes its own inefficiency.

The dishwasher became an arena of game theory. The commute became a live case study in real options. Even gossip turned into a distributed intelligence network.

So it was inevitable that *strategy itself* would be packaged and resold — as if the act of thinking could be franchised.

The self-help world doesn't sell peace; it sells **the illusion of agency.** Because people don't really want serenity — they want dashboards for serenity.

VI. Behavioral Dynamics: The Hope Economy

What keeps the self-help engine running isn't greed — it's *hope*.

Every "How to Stop Procrastinating" book works, briefly, because it *feels* like progress. Behavioral economists call this **the progress illusion** — the same phenomenon that makes people refill carts they never check out.

The average self-help consumer isn't failing. They're **iterating endlessly without shipping.**

VII. Archetypes of the Perpetual Seeker

Archetype	Typical Motto	Core Belief	Strategic Weakness
The Optimizer	"There's always a better system."	Salvation lies in scheduling.	Burns out updating Notion.
The Disciple	"My coach changed my life."	Outsources wisdom.	Forgets to self-verify.
The Collector	"I've read all 17 books."	Knowledge = transformation.	Confuses input for output.
The Cynic	"All self-help is nonsense."	Sees through everything.	Improves nothing.
The Meta-Thinker	"I'm self-helping my self-help."	Awareness equals progress.	Infinite regress.

Margin note: "The self-help journey ends where it began — with the suspicion that you never needed a journey."

VIII. Anecdote Two: The Enlightened Consultant

When *Raghav*, a management consultant, took a sabbatical to "find balance," he enrolled in a mindfulness retreat.

The retreat leader turned out to be a former consultant too — specializing in "Zen for CXOs." They discussed KPIs for detachment. PowerPoint slides included "ROI of Inner Stillness."

Raghav returned home with a certification in "Applied Tranquility." He now charges $499/hour to teach corporations how to breathe strategically.

Capitalism, it seems, can monetize even its own antidote.

IX. The Existential Undercurrent

Perhaps we buy self-help because it comforts us with **structure.** The chaos of life feels manageable when reduced to bullet points and SMART goals.

But not everything broken wants fixing. Not every emotion requires optimization.

Sometimes sadness is just a system notification: *"Humanity still functioning."*

The irony is that the more we seek to improve ourselves, the more we reinforce the belief that we are insufficient. The market doesn't create the wound — it keeps it clean enough to never heal.

X. The Strategic Countermove: Doing Life Poorly, But Honestly

After 36 essays of frameworks and metaphors, here's the un-framework: Try less. Fail slower. Laugh sooner.

Reject the idea that every flaw demands a playbook. Let inefficiency breathe.

Because real self-help isn't about "becoming your best self." It's about *being okay with your current draft version.*

XI. Cross-References: Wisdom from the Other Arcs

- From **"The Dishwasher Dilemma"**: Cooperation works better than optimization.
- From **"The Queue Theory"**: Waiting isn't wasted — it's perspective accumulating.
- From **"Brand Loyalty and Stockholm Syndrome"**: Sometimes the problem isn't the brand, it's the need to belong.
- From **"The Art of Doing Nothing"**: Stillness isn't absence of movement — it's the presence of awareness.

The real strategic synthesis of life is this: We mistake busyness for meaning, and metrics for proof. But neither dishes nor destinies get cleaner that way.

XII. The Moral (Filed Under: "Last Known Version of the Soul")

Moral: The only thing more profitable than selling happiness is selling the idea that you're almost there.

"Hope Capital Index, 2025"

Institute for Existential Economics reports: – 68% of consumers of self-help content identify as "work in progress." – 82% feel guilty for not meditating correctly. – 97% bought at least one "transformational" book in the past year. Economists define self-help as **a recurring-revenue model built on renewable despair.**

Epilogue Fragment: The Pause Between Pages

You close yet another self-help book. The last page says, *"You are enough."* You nod, satisfied — until the next notification whispers, *"Top 10 habits of people who believe they're enough."*

You smile, exhausted, enlightened, and faintly amused. You know the truth now: Growth isn't a ladder — it's a loop. And you, dear reader, are the product and the market, both.

CHAPTER XXXVIII

AI, LIFE COACHES, AND THE OUTSOURCING OF THINKING

Or: Automation of judgment and the end of original confusion.

I. The Situation

It begins innocently enough. You ask your virtual assistant to remind you to drink water. Then to meditate. Then, one day, to decide whether you should quit your job.

The algorithm hesitates, then responds:

"That depends on your long-term career goals and personal values."

You nod, impressed. A decade ago, only your therapist and that one insufferable friend from business school could sound that smugly reasonable.

Now, the same advice arrives without judgment — and without a soul.

Somewhere between "Hey Siri" and "Who am I really?", we stopped thinking *with* tools and started thinking *through* them.

II. The Model: The Automation Ladder of Cognition

AI and the life-coaching economy are two sides of the same existential coin: both exist because modern humans can't stand the burden of self-direction.

We've built a hierarchy of cognitive outsourcing that looks suspiciously like a corporate org chart.

Tier	Function	Example	Cognitive Impact
Level 1	Automate memory	Reminders, notes	Externalized recall
Level 2	Automate analysis	Recommender systems	Pattern delegation
Level 3	Automate judgment	AI-driven "life advice"	Outsourced discernment
Level 4	Automate meaning	Spiritual coaches, prompts	Surrender of autonomy

What started as convenience evolved into **existential dependency.** We no longer just use systems — we consult them for moral calibration.

III. Anecdotal Case Study: The Algorithmic Guru

Rina was tired of dating, tired of therapy, and especially tired of decisions. So she turned to an AI-powered "life optimization" app called **Clarity.AI**.

The app analyzed her texts, sleep patterns, and Spotify history, then suggested:

"You are experiencing emotional redundancy. Consider pivoting to a purpose-driven lifestyle."

It sounded profound. She immediately subscribed.

Six weeks later, she began referring to herself as "a beta version of my next self." Her friends noticed she now spoke entirely in bullet points.

Her thinking wasn't wrong — it was *formatted.*

IV. Cross-Reference: The Ghost of the Strategy Deck

Back in **"The First Date Pitch Deck"**, we saw how romance became a slide presentation. Now, even selfhood has adopted a similar syntax — measurable, pitchable, downloadable.

We've replaced "Who am I?" with "What's my user profile?" Existence, once a mystery, is now a dashboard.

Figure 1: The diminishing returns of algorithmic authenticity.

And somewhere in the boardroom of being, *AI is the new self-help coach — cheaper, faster, never tired, and infinitely agreeable.*

V. Behavioral Dynamics: The Comfort of Delegated Thought

Cognitive offloading is seductive because it **feels like intelligence while bypassing effort.** Behavioral psychology identifies several biases that make this outsourcing irresistible:

- **Automation Bias:** Trusting systems over self because they *seem objective.*
- **Choice Fatigue:** Delegating moral decisions to preserve mental bandwidth.
- **Confirmation Comfort:** AI curates advice that flatters existing biases.
- **Pseudo-Reflection:** Mistaking recommendation for reflection.

We no longer wrestle with dilemmas; we scroll through their summaries.

VI. Archetypes of the Outsourced Mind

Archetype	Typical Motto	Strategic Payoff	Existential Cost
The Delegator	"The system knows best."	Decision relief	Identity dilution
The Optimizer	"There's an app for that."	Time efficiency	Loss of intuition
The Coach Collector	"I have three mentors and one chatbot."	External validation	No inner compass
The AI Whisperer	"It really *gets* me."	Parasitic intimacy	Simulated empathy
The Analog Rebel	"I still think for myself."	Authenticity	Chronic uncertainty

🗨 *Margin note:* "Humans once envied gods for omniscience. Now they envy algorithms for decisiveness."

VII. Anecdote Two: The Executive and the Algorithm

Rajiv, a senior VP, faced a merger decision that could affect 3,000 employees. He fed key data into an AI decision engine for "neutral guidance." The system generated a 40-page strategy memo — complete with ethical analysis and sensitivity mapping.

He followed it. The merger failed spectacularly.

When asked by the board what went wrong, he replied:

"It was statistically sound."

And there, in that single phrase, lies the quiet tragedy of our times: **the abdication of judgment in exchange for justification.**

VIII. The Corporate Parallel: From Human Capital to Cognitive Automation

Corporates were the first to pioneer thought outsourcing — through consultants, dashboards, and "executive summaries." AI merely democratized it.

We used to hire analysts to interpret complexity. Now, we hire algorithms to reduce it to a digestible narrative — one we can pretend we authored.

The tragedy isn't automation. It's **the death of deliberation.** Thinking used to hurt. Now it just scrolls.

IX. Cross-References: Echoes Across the Arcs

- From **"Queue Theory and Supermarket Strategy"**: Patience reveals patterns that haste conceals — but AI never waits.
- From **"Parenting as Change Management"**: Real growth involves resistance; automation removes it.
- From **"Brand Loyalty and Stockholm Syndrome"**: Dependence feels like trust when dressed as convenience.
- From **"The Art of Doing Nothing"**: True thought requires stillness — something no system can simulate.

The pattern is unmistakable: Every domain we optimize loses a piece of its humanity. The more efficient the system, the less it needs *you.*

X. The Existential Undercurrent: The Hollowing of Choice

Philosophers once defined being human as the capacity to choose. Now, we call it "decision fatigue."

We've turned freedom into a UX problem. The modern self doesn't think — it *curates.*

When Nietzsche said "God is dead," he didn't foresee that we'd replace Him with a recommendation engine. And worse — that we'd like it.

XI. The Strategic Countermove: Reclaiming Unassisted Thinking

There is a radical act left: **to think without prompts.**

To sit with a question and not Google it. To make a decision without data validation. To risk being wrong — beautifully, humanly wrong.

Judgment, after all, is not the act of knowing perfectly, but of *owning imperfection consciously.*

Maybe wisdom in the AI age is not superior cognition, but deliberate *uncertainty.*

XII. The Moral (Filed Under: "Terms of Conscious Use")

Moral: Intelligence is no longer rare — the courage to use it is.

> **"Cognitive Outsourcing Index, 2025"**
>
> *Institute for Algorithmic Ethics reports:* – 79% of adults "consult technology before making life decisions." – 62% trust AI more than peers for relationship advice. – 48% of coaches now use AI-generated feedback for clients. Eco nomists define modern cognition as **a subscription-based service with declining self-involvement.**

Epilogue Fragment: The Silence of the Prompt

One day, you'll ask your digital assistant a question it can't answer — something like, *"Am I doing this right?"*

And for a moment, there will be silence. The servers will hum. The signal will fail.

And in that gap — brief, analog, terrifying — you might feel something ancient returning.

The forgotten sound of your own thoughts.

CHAPTER XXXIX

THE GYM MEMBERSHIP PROBLEM

> *Or: Commitment devices and the illusion of progress.*

I. The Situation

January 2nd. You walk into the gym — earnest, resolute, carrying a brand-new water bottle and the faint smell of self-improvement.

The receptionist smiles the way a car dealer does when you pick the *extended warranty*. You pay for the annual plan — the "Smart Saver Package," which guarantees both fiscal responsibility and eventual guilt.

By February, you've been there twice. By March, you've switched to "home workouts." By April, your home workouts have switched to *Netflix marathons in athleisure wear.*

And by June, you're renewing anyway — because **hope renews faster than habits.**

II. The Model: The Economics of Abandoned Intention

Behavioral economists call it a **commitment device** — a mechanism that helps align your future behavior with your present resolve. The gym membership is the most elegant example: *you prepay for your guilt in bulk.*

Variable	Economic Term	Psychological Equivalent
Membership Fee	Sunk Cost	Self-worth investment
Attendance	Marginal Utility	Diminishing enthusiasm
Renewal	Future Discounting	Optimism bias
Mirror Selfies	Vanity Metrics	KPI for delusion

In pure microeconomic terms, the gym is a subscription model monetizing **human inconsistency.**

III. Anecdotal Case Study: The Treadmill That Waited

Meet *Ankit*, a 33-year-old data analyst who joined a premium fitness chain "to invest in himself." He bought running shoes, a smartwatch, and protein powder with the solemnity of a man entering sainthood.

He visited thrice.

By week four, his smartwatch began displaying a passive-aggressive message: *"Still alive?"* By month two, he began avoiding the gym road altogether. By month six, he started referring to it as "a sunk cost lesson."

He never canceled the membership. Why? Because canceling would *make it real.*

Behavioral scientists call this **the sunk cost fallacy.** But in human terms, it's **emotional EMI for good intentions.**

IV. The Behavioral Dynamics: Sweating Without Moving

Every treadmill is a metaphor for the modern mind — loud, expensive, and stationary.

The gym membership operates on a delicate web of psychological traps:

- **Optimism Bias:** "This year will be different."
- **Planning Fallacy:** "I'll go thrice a week."
- **Loss Aversion:** "I can't cancel; I already paid."
- **Identity Signaling:** "At least I *have* a gym membership."
- **Reward Substitution:** "Buying gear feels like progress."

Together, these biases form what we might call **The Wellness Ponzi Scheme:** Your present self borrows moral credit from your future self, who inevitably defaults.

V. Cross-Reference: The Subscription Overload Problem

Back in **Chapter 20**, we examined how digital subscriptions trap you in a low-grade fiscal Stockholm Syndrome. The gym is the analog equivalent — only sweatier.

Both monetize *hope deferred.* Both rely on the principle of invisible usage. And both, conveniently, auto-renew.

The business model of modern life, it seems, is **charging rent on our future selves.**

VI. Archetypes of the Modern Exerciser

Archetype	Motto	Strategic Strength	Weakness
The January Enthusiast	"New year, new me!"	Explosive start	Dies by February
The Equipment Hoarder	"I'll set up a home gym."	Strong purchasing power	Uses clothes rack as squat stand
The Social Gymmer	"I go for the vibes."	Networker	Treats workout as background noise
The Data Devotee	"If it's not tracked, it didn't happen."	Quantified discipline	Forgets to feel
The Existential Walker	"Steps count as cardio."	Sustainable approach	Never sweats

🗨 *Margin note:* "Discipline begins when the playlist ends."

VII. Anecdote Two: The Corporate Fitness Analogy

Consider *Maya*, an HR manager who introduced a "Wellness at Work" program. Employees could log steps for rewards — gift vouchers, shoutouts, and one fateful golden dumbbell trophy.

Participation soared for a week. Then the data showed 20 employees "averaging 45,000 steps per day." All while working from home.

The system was gamed, the data was doctored, and the dumbbell went to Finance.

Maya realized too late: **metrics without meaning breed performance without purpose.**

Which, incidentally, also describes most gym routines.

VIII. Cross-References: Strategic Parallels from Everyday Life

- From **"The Weekend Project Fallacy"**: Overestimating motivation and underestimating pain — the twin pillars of delusion.
- From **"The Art of Doing Nothing"**: Rest is productive — provided you've done something to rest from.
- From **"The Self-Help Industrial Complex"**: The gym is simply a physical manifestation of self-improvement capitalism.
- From **"The Great Commute Game"**: Efficiency without purpose still goes nowhere — only faster.

It all connects. Your dumbbells are your dashboards. Your treadmill is your email inbox. Both simulate progress through movement, not meaning.

IX. The Existential Undercurrent: The Mirage of Measured Growth

The tragedy of the modern age is that we've replaced *transformation* with *tracking*. We don't want to change; we want to monitor the idea of changing.

It's the same energy that makes us check our sleep score after a bad night, as if data could redeem fatigue. We've turned the act of becoming into an administrative task.

But the body doesn't care about graphs — it only remembers motion. And the soul? It only counts laughter disguised as breathlessness.

X. The Strategic Countermove: The Unquantified Workout

Here's a radical idea: Go for a walk without your phone. Do ten pushups without logging them. Stretch because it feels good, not because your app approves.

Stop treating fitness like a portfolio to optimize. Be gloriously inefficient. Sweat without spreadsheets.

The only KPI worth chasing is **joy per minute.**

XI. The Moral (Filed Under: "Deferred Gratification and Deferred Gratitude")

Moral: Paying for progress isn't the same as making it.

Or, as the great philosopher of unused gym towels once said:

"A treadmill is just an expensive guilt loop."

"Wellness Economics, 2025"

Institute for Behavioral Health Finance reports: – 63% of annual gym memberships go unused past the third month. – 81% of subscribers claim "I'll start next week." – 12% believe purchasing workout shoes burns calories. Behavioral economists define fitness spending as **a recurring donation to the religion of future discipline.**

Epilogue Fragment: The Abandoned Locker Key

Months later, you find your gym locker key at the bottom of a drawer. You hold it up, like an artifact from a past civilization — one that believed in redemption through sweat.

You smile. Then you order biryani. Balance, after all, is also fitness.

CHAPTER XL

VACATION PLANNING AND THE ILLUSION OF CONTROL

Or: Forecast errors and overfitting the itinerary.

I. The Situation

Vacations, in theory, are about freedom. In practice, they are PowerPoint presentations disguised as leisure.

You open Excel — sorry, "Google Sheets" — to build an itinerary. Columns include *Date, Time, Activity, Distance, Cost,* and *Emotional Fulfilment (TBD).*

Somewhere between "Breakfast at 8:00 a.m." and "Relaxing Beach Time, 9:45–10:15," you realize: you've project-managed joy.

The modern traveler doesn't seek serenity — they seek **control that looks like serenity.**

II. The Model: Forecasting Fun in an Unstable System

Vacation planning operates like a corporate forecasting exercise. You assume that variables (weather, mood, spouse) are predictable and controllable. They are not.

Variable	Forecasted	Actual	Explanation
Weather	"Sunny and mild"	Tropical storm	Nature ignored your spreadsheet
Family Mood	"Cheerful"	Mutinous	Insufficient snack reserves
Sightseeing Efficiency	"6 attractions/ day"	"One museum and an argument"	Human bandwidth exceeded
Budget	"₹35,000"	"₹35,000 by Day 2"	Inflation + ice cream

Planning gives the illusion of foresight, much like stock analysts "predicting" markets after they've already closed.

III. Anecdotal Case Study: The Itinerary Industrialist

Meet *Rohit,* a management consultant who planned his family's 8-day Europe trip with the precision of a military campaign. He used conditional formatting to highlight "critical dependencies" (e.g., "Pack kids before leaving hotel"). His itinerary was shared in real time via Slack.

By Day 3, the family revolted. By Day 5, his 12-tab travel sheet had a new name: *"The Prison of Joy.xlsx."*

On the flight home, he sighed and said, "Next time, I'll build contingencies." That's when his wife whispered the truth every planner dreads:

"Next time, we're going without you."

IV. The Strategy Concept: Overfitting the Itinerary

In data science, **overfitting** happens when a model performs beautifully on known data but fails miserably in real-world conditions. Vacation planning is exactly that: it optimizes for an *ideal version of your family that doesn't exist.*

The model assumes everyone wakes up on time, nobody argues about food, and Wi-Fi works in the mountains.

It's a flawless plan — until reality introduces *children, humidity, and human emotion.*

Overfitting joy is the surest way to underperform at happiness.

V. Behavioral Economics of the Holiday Planner

Vacation planning brings out the worst of our behavioral biases — or, to be fair, *the most entertaining.*

- **Control Illusion:** Believing you can schedule spontaneity.
- **Planning Fallacy:** Underestimating travel time, overestimating patience.
- **Sunk Cost Effect:** "We have to see the 4th temple; we *paid* for the taxi."
- **Social Comparison:** "Their Maldives looked more turquoise."
- **Post-Decision Dissonance:** Defending your miserable experience as "authentic."

Each bias conspires to make leisure indistinguishable from labor — just in shorts.

VI. Cross-Reference: The Commute and the Cosmos

If you recall **"The Great Commute Game,"** traffic was a metaphor for uncertainty under constrained rationality.

Vacation travel is that — but with sunscreen and emotional baggage.

Similarly, **"The Umbrella Hedge Fund"** taught us that risk cannot be eliminated, only priced. Vacation insurance is the same idea: a polite way of admitting defeat before departure.

And from **"The Self-Help Industrial Complex"**, we learned that the pursuit of peace can itself be exhausting. Planning a vacation, then, is the ultimate form of self-help hypocrisy — scheduling liberation.

VII. Anecdote Two: The Couple Who Spreadsheeted Love

Meera and *Vikram* were newly married. For their honeymoon, they decided to visit Greece.

Each day was broken into "romantic moments" (column F) and "Instagram potential" (column G). They had a rule: at least three "authentic experiences" per day.

On Day 4, exhausted, they found themselves arguing over whether the sunset at Santorini was "authentic enough."

It was then, amid golden light and mutual irritation, that they achieved something resembling enlightenment: They stopped photographing, started laughing, and — in a rare triumph of strategy — abandoned the plan.

VIII. The Corporate Parallel: Project Management and the Mirage of Predictability

Corporate life is full of vacation planners in disguise. We call them "Program Managers."

Every Gantt chart, every sprint, every OKR is a kind of existential itinerary — an attempt to impose order on the absurd. And just like a family vacation, the deliverables keep slipping, the budget bloats, and someone always cries in public.

The deeper truth: **Planning is not control — it's choreography for chaos.**

We don't plan to succeed. We plan to comfort ourselves while failing gracefully.

IX. The Existential Undercurrent: The Fragility of Foresight

Every trip is a small rehearsal for life — you build expectations, pack for contingencies, and still forget the one thing you really needed.

Planning gives you the illusion of mastery, but travel — like existence — reminds you that mastery is a myth. The weather will change, the road will flood, the museum will close, and you will laugh anyway.

Because the point was never control. It was *participation.*

X. The Strategic Countermove: The Art of Planned Surrender

The solution isn't abandoning plans — it's designing for *graceful failure.*

Make itineraries loose enough for accidents. Budget for detours. Leave one day gloriously blank — a holiday for the holiday.

In corporate terms: build *slack* into your life's schedule. In poetic terms: allow serendipity to RSVP.

XI. The Moral (Filed Under: "Forecasting Fun in an Uncooperative Universe")

Moral: Control is the comfort food of anxious minds — satisfying, familiar, and nutritionally empty.

Or, as a great traveler once didn't say:

"If you want to make God laugh, show Him your travel plan."

> **"Vacation Economics, 2025"**
>
> *Institute for Predictive Leisure Studies reports:* – 76% of travelers experience "planner's remorse." – 52% admit to post-vacation burnout. – 89% of family trips feature at least one "emotional bottleneck." Economists define travel planning as **forecasting happiness in stochastic conditions with zero governance controls.**

Epilogue Fragment: The Missed Train and the Found Moment

On the last day of your trip, you miss the train — of course. You sit on the platform, sweating, luggage leaning against your shin. No Wi-Fi, no plan, no urgency.

A child laughs nearby. Someone hums a tune. You breathe.

And for a brief, brilliant moment — you experience what you were planning for all along: **unmanaged peace.**

CHAPTER XLI

THE EXISTENTIAL KPI

> *Or: Measuring what can't (and shouldn't) be measured.*

I. The Situation

Every performance review season, somewhere in a fluorescent-lit conference room, someone asks:

"But what's the metric for happiness?"

You chuckle. They don't.

And so begins humanity's most persistent delusion — that **everything meaningful must be measurable**, and everything measurable must therefore be meaningful.

The corporate world has weaponized metrics; the personal world has adopted them. Your morning walk has a "step count," your meditation app rates your calmness, your relationships have "engagement levels," and your mood is an "insight."

The spreadsheet has eaten the soul.

II. The Model: The Metricization of Meaning

Let's define a framework — because if we're going to mock it, we might as well formalize it.

Domain	Original Purpose	Current KPI	Measurement Tool
Work	Value creation	"OKRs achieved"	Dashboard
Fitness	Well-being	"Calories burned"	Wearable
Relationships	Love, trust	"Texts replied within 3 mins"	Read receipts
Spirituality	Presence	"Streak count"	App notification
Self-worth	Contentment	"Likes and follows"	Social media

What began as structure has become surveillance. We've transformed introspection into analytics — *a quantified introspection economy.*

III. Anecdotal Case Study: The KPI of Inner Peace

Meet *Karan*, a senior marketing manager turned reluctant philosopher. After a mild burnout, he took a "spiritual sabbatical" (read: unpaid leave with better hashtags).

He tracked everything — meditation minutes, gratitude entries, even frequency of "moments of awe."

By month two, his spreadsheet showed 28% more calm and 11% less envy. He felt great — until he realized he was now *stressed about maintaining his calmness metrics.*

"I think I'm failing at peace," he told his therapist.

Thus was born the modern condition: **anxiety about relaxation.**

IV. The Strategy Concept: Metric Myopia

In management theory, **metric myopia** occurs when measurement replaces meaning. You start optimizing for what's countable, not what counts.

In organizations, this leads to *vanity metrics.* In life, it leads to *vanity itself.*

The moment you ask, "Am I growing as a person?" and expect a chart — the problem isn't the answer. It's that you believed one existed.

V. Behavioral Economics of Existential Accounting

The compulsion to measure everything is not random; it's behavioral economics in yoga pants.

- **Control Illusion:** Measurement feels like mastery.
- **Availability Heuristic:** What's measurable feels real; what's ineffable feels suspicious.
- **Loss Aversion:** We'd rather track progress than risk regression.
- **Signaling:** Sharing metrics = proof of virtue.
- **Temporal Myopia:** Long-term meaning gets discounted for short-term validation.

We have, in effect, built **a behavioral market for the soul** — trading purpose futures at the price of presence.

VI. Cross-Reference: Lessons from Previous Arcs

- From **"The Umbrella Hedge Fund"**, we learned that uncertainty can't be eliminated — only acknowledged. The same goes for meaning.
- From **"The Social Media Strategy Spiral"**, the self became a brand. The KPI, inevitably, became *attention.*

- From **"Minimalism as a Maximalist Strategy"**, we discovered that simplicity, too, can be performed — quantified minimalism is maximal irony.
- From **"The Art of Doing Nothing"**, we learned the rare wisdom of slack — immeasurable, inefficient, irreplaceable.

The throughline is unmistakable: our obsession with metrics is not a quest for clarity, but for comfort — a defense mechanism against ambiguity.

VII. Anecdote Two: The Company That Measured Everything

A mid-sized tech firm once tried to apply "data-driven mindfulness" across its workforce. Each employee wore biometric sensors that tracked heart rate, calmness, and emotional tone during meetings.

For a week, everyone was angelic. By week two, people began gaming the system — taking deep breaths during arguments to maintain "calmness scores." By week four, HR proudly announced:

"Emotional well-being improved by 17%!"

By week five, everyone hated each other quietly.

It turns out, **quantified calmness is just well-documented repression.**

VIII. The Corporate Parallel: When Metrics Mutiny

Every organization eventually becomes a hostage to its KPIs. They start as tools of insight and end as instruments of tyranny.

When your team starts optimizing *for the metric itself* — rather than the outcome — you've crossed the line from management to mimicry.

In personal life, this looks like pretending to be happy because your "mood tracker" said you were. In corporate life, it's pretending to innovate because the "innovation index" said so.

The map is not the meaning.

IX. The Existential Undercurrent: The Fear Beneath the Formula

Why do we measure meaning? Because we're afraid it won't exist unless verified.

Numbers are comforting; ambiguity is terrifying. We'd rather be precisely wrong than vaguely right.

But life's value resists metrics for the same reason love resists logic — it's not a system; it's a story. You can audit a process. You can't audit purpose.

X. The Strategic Countermove: The KPI of Unmeasurables

Here's the paradox: the things that make life *work* are precisely those that don't *count.*

Kindness. Wonder. Patience. Laughter. They don't scale, they don't forecast, and they never trend on dashboards.

Try tracking "moments of grace." The data will always be incomplete — and that's the point.

The counter-strategy, then, is **qualitative living**: practicing presence without performance.

If you must have a KPI, let it be:

"How many times today did I forget to check the time?"

XI. The Moral (Filed Under: "Vanity Metrics of the Soul")

Moral: Not everything that can be measured matters; not everything that matters can survive being measured.

Or as the Prophet of PowerPoint once said:

"Happiness doesn't fit on a slide."

"The Quantified Self Economy, 2025"

Institute for Cognitive Metrics reports: – 78% of adults track at least one mood-related statistic. – 63% say they "feel anxious" when not tracking progress. – 91% have no idea what progress actually means. Economists define existential measurement as **a productivity trap disguised as enlightenment.**

Epilogue Fragment: The Unticked Box

Late one night, you scroll through your task manager. Everything is checked off — emails, errands, even "self-care."

And yet, something feels unfinished.

You stare at the blank space between items — the untracked, the unoptimized, the alive. And for once, you close the app without adding "Be present" to the list.

Because maybe, finally, you are.

CHAPTER XLII

THE GRAND STRATEGY OF DOING LIFE POORLY, BUT WITH STYLE

Or: Synthesis, self-deprecation, and surrender.

I. The Situation

At some point between *The Dishwasher Dilemma* and *The Existential KPI*, you've probably noticed a pattern: everyone is improvising, nobody is winning, and the PowerPoint of life keeps crashing mid-presentation.

And yet, we persist.

We make plans, chase purpose, and benchmark happiness — all while suspecting that the game is rigged. Still, we show up. Because showing up badly still beats not showing up at all.

This chapter is for those who've tried to live strategically, only to find that life refuses to cooperate — the professionals of imperfection. The accidental philosophers. The stylishly defeated.

II. The Model: Life as an Unwinnable Game

If strategy is about aligning limited resources to achieve specific goals, then life is a study in **constant misalignment.**

Variable	Strategic Ideal	Actual Outcome	Commentary
Resources	Time, talent, temperament	Never enough of any	"Optimization pending."
Goals	Clear, measurable	Shifting, emotional	"Scope creep in progress."
Feedback Loops	Immediate and actionable	Ambiguous and delayed	"Quarterly meaning review overdue."
Success Metric	Fulfillment	Maintenance of dignity	"At least you tried."

By corporate standards, existence is a loss-making venture. And yet, by human standards, it's the only investment worth continuing.

III. Anecdotal Case Study: The Strategist's Midlife Off-site

Imagine *Ananya*, 44, head of strategy at a mid-sized conglomerate. She has spent two decades modeling markets, forecasting volatility, and managing uncertainty with spreadsheets that could humble NASA.

But at home, her teenage daughter won't take her advice, her plants keep dying, and her dog loves her husband more.

One night, in an uncharacteristic act of surrender, she closes her laptop, opens a bottle of wine, and decides to "let the quarter go."

She ends up dancing — badly — in the living room. Her daughter laughs. For the first time in months, Ananya experiences what her dashboards never captured: *joy unmeasured.*

That, right there, is **strategic incompetence as liberation.**

IV. The Synthesis: Learning from Failure Across the Arcs

Across these 41 absurdities masquerading as essays, a through-line has emerged. Let's pretend it's deliberate.

- From **"The Dishwasher Dilemma"**, we learned that cooperation beats competition — unless you're arguing about detergent.
- From **"Kitchen Politics"**, that every family dinner is a micro-MBA in resource allocation.
- From **"The Weekend Project Fallacy"**, that optimism is just delusion with better branding.
- From **"The Great Commute Game"**, that traffic is the universe's performance review system.
- From **"The WhatsApp Mini-Ecosystem"**, that information sharing doesn't equal communication.
- From **"Brand Loyalty and Stockholm Syndrome"**, that marketing works best when you're emotionally kidnapped.
- From **"Relationship Portfolio Management"**, that diversification doesn't apply to affection.
- From **"The Existential KPI"**, that measurement is just bureaucracy for the soul.

And from all of them, collectively, we learned this: **there is no unified field theory of existence.** Just a series of partial insights, sarcastic epiphanies, and occasional good days.

V. The Strategy Concept: Inefficient Excellence

In military doctrine, there's a term called *Mission Command* — giving soldiers clear intent, then trusting them to improvise when reality refuses to comply.

Life, as it turns out, operates the same way. You can't optimize every moment. You can only set intent, then surrender stylishly when chaos laughs at you.

The grand strategy, therefore, isn't mastery. It's *competent chaos management with aesthetic flair.*

You won't always win — but you can fail with rhythm.

VI. Behavioral Economics of Graceful Failure

We humans are irrational, loss-averse, and mildly ridiculous. But those traits, inconvenient as they are, create resilience.

- **Loss Aversion:** Keeps us sentimental enough to stay.
- **Status Quo Bias:** Helps us endure.
- **Confirmation Bias:** Allows us to believe it's all fine (until coffee).
- **Optimism Bias:** Persuades us to try again tomorrow.

If we were fully rational, we'd have given up by now. It's our cognitive errors that make us love, laugh, and keep showing up for disappointment with punctuality.

Our irrationality is our operating system — inefficient, but beautiful.

VII. Cross-References: The Wisdom of the Broken

- From **"The Art of Doing Nothing"** — sometimes stillness is the only progress left.
- From **"The Gym Membership Problem"** — effort is admirable, even if misdirected.
- From **"Vacation Planning and the Illusion of Control"** — failure is often just spontaneity misinterpreted.
- From **"Parenting as Change Management"** — people resist growth because it's exhausting.

- From **"The Neighborhood Gossip Network"** — most complex systems function not despite chaos, but because of it.

The world's best strategies are post-rationalized accidents. And so are we.

VIII. Anecdote Two: The Philosopher at the Supermarket

There's an old man who shops at the same grocery store every Sunday. He takes forever — double-checks prices, compares brands, sighs loudly at the yogurt aisle.

When asked why he moves so slowly, he says, "Because speed isn't the same as efficiency, and I have nothing to optimize anymore."

Then he grins. That's what enlightenment looks like now — a pensioner buying tomatoes without hurry.

IX. The Existential Undercurrent: Style as the Last Strategy

We cannot control outcomes, but we can control *how we miss them.* Grace, humor, and self-deprecation are the only currencies that hold value across crises.

Style, in this sense, is not superficial — it's philosophical. It's how we signal defiance to chaos. It's how we reclaim dignity from disorder.

To "do life poorly but with style" is to accept the futility and still curate the playlist.

X. The Strategic Countermove: Intent Without Illusion

So here's the final framework — the anti-framework:

1. **Set Intent.** Begin with sincerity.
2. **Stay Playful.** Treat every plan as an experiment.
3. **Expect Error.** Failure is feedback disguised as irony.
4. **Extract Humor.** Sarcasm is emotional diversification.
5. **Leave Space.** Because serendipity needs oxygen.

It's not mastery. It's choreography with gravity.

XI. The Moral (Filed Under: "Strategic Futility with Panache")

Moral: Life's not about doing it well — it's about doing it *deliberately badly* with enough wit to make the gods laugh instead of interfere.

Or as the great uncredited philosopher of aisle four once said:

"Perfection is a boring endgame. Mediocrity, done consciously, is art."

"Existential Economics, 2025"

The Institute of Strategic Futility reports: – 94% of adults suspect they're improvising. – 82% pretend it's intentional. – 100% are right. Behavioral analysts define self-deprecating humor as **the last efficient coping mechanism in late capitalism.**

Epilogue Fragment: The Laugh Track at the End of the Universe

You wake up one day — older, softer, unoptimized. The inbox still overflows. The dishes still exist. The Wi-Fi still drops. And yet — the light slants differently.

You make coffee, badly. You hum something tuneless. And as the world whirs with dashboards and deadlines, you realize:

The strategy was never to win. It was to *notice.*

And for once, noticing feels like enough.

CLOSING NOTE

CLOSING NOTE

In Gratitude to Chaos (and Other Unwitting Collaborators)
(Acknowledgments for "Strategy in Everyday Life")

The Thank-You Section That Accidentally Became a Confession

It is customary at the end of a book to thank those who made it possible. But the truth is, no one *makes* a book like this possible. It simply… happens — like a budget overrun or an unplanned child.

Still, in the spirit of professional accountability and emotional debt settlement, some acknowledgments are due.

To the Invisible Board of Directors

To **Nameeta** - who provided the case studies I never asked for. You are the original faculty of this domestic MBA — masters of negotiation, masters of escalation, and frequent contributors to "The Dishwasher Dilemma." Every eye-roll was peer review; every argument, a strategy sprint.

To my **friends**, who inspired "The Social Supply Chain" and "The Favor Bank," usually by borrowing things and never returning them. You taught me that reciprocity is a theory, not a law.

To my **colleagues**, who made "The Relationship Economy" essays possible simply by existing in open-plan offices. Your synergy, like your coffee, was both motivating and mildly burnt.

And to my **extended family**, who personified "The Stakeholder Matrix" so vividly that Harvard might request a licensing fee.

To the Enablers of Everyday Madness

To the **commute**, for teaching me that time is both linear and circular, depending on the traffic signal.

To **Wi-Fi**, whose intermittent existence ensured I could never fully escape work or fully access peace.

To **algorithms**, for deciding what I wanted before I knew it myself. Your predictive arrogance kept me humble — and subscribed.

To **customer service chatbots**, for proving that empathy can, indeed, be automated — badly.

And to **coffee**, the liquid OKR of the modern soul — aligning energy and anxiety since the industrial revolution.

To My Philosophical Adversaries

To all the management thinkers — Sun Tzu, Porter, Drucker, Christensen — whose frameworks I borrowed, bent, and occasionally broke. I suspect you did not intend your ideas to explain why someone refuses to load the dishwasher, but we live in flexible times.

To behavioral economists — Kahneman, Thaler, Ariely — thank you for proving that humans are predictably irrational. It's been the only KPI I've consistently met.

To my at-home therapist, who kindly pointed out that sarcasm is not a sustainable coping mechanism. We'll have to agree to disagree.

To the Unpaid Intern Known as the Universe

You, chaotic architect of coincidence and entropy, are the real co-author here. You sent the traffic jams, the flight delays, the WhatsApp notifications at 2 a.m., the existential dread at

4 p.m., and the clarity at 11:37 on a Tuesday when I least deserved it.

Every time I thought I was managing my life, you introduced a system crash. Every time I tried to make meaning, you sent memes.

You're terrible at following instructions, but an excellent teacher.

To the Readers (Strategists in Denial)

You, dear reader, are the last stakeholder in this overextended metaphor.

If you came here for genuine self-help, I apologize. If you came for mockery disguised as philosophy, you're home.

You are the ultimate case study: a rational being making irrational choices, beautifully. And if you've made it this far — through dishwashers, commutes, algorithms, heartbreaks, and brand loyalties — then you've demonstrated the only skill that really matters in strategy or in life: *persistence despite nonsense.*

You're my favorite kind of strategist — the one who fails forward, with a smirk.

The Final Audit

After 42 essays, 126 frameworks, and an incalculable number of sighs, here's the only metric that matters:

Deliverable	Status
Clarity	Overdue
Control	Revoked
Humor	Achieved (intermittently)
Meaning	Emergent property of exhaustion

Everything else — like most OKRs — can be "revisited next quarter."

Postscript: The Optional Toast

If you're reading this late at night, take a moment. Close the book. Look around at your half-finished plans, your slightly overcooked dreams, your mismatched ambitions.

Congratulations. You're doing it wrong — and that's exactly right.

Here's to the glorious inefficiency of being human: the typos, the tangents, the triumphs that look like accidents. Here's to bad plans, good jokes, and decent coffee. Here's to doing life poorly — but with unmistakable style.

LIST OF KEY FRAMEWORKS & MODELS

(Compiled by the Office of Everyday Strategy, Department of Practical Futility)

"All models are wrong. Some are entertaining." — Anonymous Strategist, probably in denial.

1. **The Dishwasher Dilemma Framework (DDF)**
   Field of Application: Domestic Game Theory **Summary:** A cooperative-competitive model explaining why two rational adults can both "plan to do it later" until entropy wins. **Key Variables:** Perceived fairness, passive aggression, and sponge moisture. **Outcome:** Always suboptimal, occasionally sparkling.
2. **Porter's Five Forks Model (PFF)**
   Field of Application: Kitchen Politics **Summary:** Adapts Porter's Five Forces to domestic power dynamics. **Forces include:**
   - Threat of new recipes (innovation fatigue),
   - Bargaining power of picky eaters,
   - Supplier leverage of grocery shoppers,
   - Competitive rivalry among amateur chefs,
   - Risk of substitutes (takeout). **Outcome:** Dinner delayed; egos sautéed.
3. **The In-Law Matrix (ILM)**
   Field of Application: Stakeholder Management **Summary:** A two-by-two grid mapping influence vs. emotional volatility. **Quadrants include:** "Supportive Advisors," "Silent Observers," "Loud Opponents," and "Diplomatic Time Bombs." **Recommended Strategy:** Mitigate exposure through diversionary grandchildren.

4. **The Weekend Project Fallacy (WPF)**
Field of Application: Behavioral Economics **Summary:** A sunk-cost framework for explaining why humans overestimate time, skill, and structural integrity. **Equation:** Confidence $\propto$ (Hours since YouTube tutorial). **Outcome:** One unfinished shelf; one finished argument.
5. **The Sibling Market Segmentation Theory (SMST)**
Field of Application: Family Economics **Summary:** Children as competing brands under a single parent corporation. **Insight:** Differentiation occurs through niche performance and selective trauma.
6. **The Umbrella Hedge Fund (UHF)**
Field of Application: Risk Mitigation **Summary:** A decision tree for evaluating the cost-benefit of carrying or not carrying an umbrella. **Result:** Carrying → No rain. Not carrying → Biblical flood. **Conclusion:** Weather gods are active portfolio managers.
7. **The Queue Management Anxiety Model (Q-MAM)**
Field of Application: Behavioral Operations **Summary:** Quantifies emotional turbulence caused by perceiving the "other line" moving faster. **Finding:** Switching queues increases regret by 237%.
8. **The WhatsApp Ecosystem Model (WEM)**
Field of Application: Social Systems Design **Summary:** A closed-loop information network optimized for notification fatigue. **Core Dynamics:** Signaling, status competition, and meme-based trust building. **Control Variable:** The "Mute for 1 Year" button.
9. **The Favor Bank Liquidity Framework (FBLF)**
Field of Application: Social Finance **Summary:** Reciprocity operates like a volatile currency with low conversion rates and high inflation. **Insight:** Emotional IOUs mature slower than guilt.
10. **The Brand Loyalty Captivity Curve (BLCC)**
Field of Application: Consumer Psychology **Summary:** Models customer attachment as a psychological hostage

situation. **Key Factors:** Habit strength, sunk cost, and logo-induced nostalgia. **Strategic Escape:** Rare, and often replaced by new captivity.

11. **The Subscription Overload Diversification Index (SODI)**
    Field of Application: Personal Finance **Summary:** Applies portfolio theory to monthly micro-subscriptions that cumulatively erode liquidity. **Equation:** Awareness = 1 / (Number of active subscriptions). **Risk Mitigation:** Denial.
12. **The Dating App Network Effect Model (DANEM)**
    Field of Application: Platform Economics **Summary:** Explains diminishing marginal returns in multi-sided romantic marketplaces. **Observation:** Each new user increases chaos faster than compatibility.
13. **The Marital BATNA Continuum (MBC)**
    Field of Application: Negotiation Strategy **Summary:** Maps the balance between assertiveness and sofa occupancy. **Optimal Zone:** Mutually Assured Forgiveness (MAF).
14. **The Emotional Labor Value Chain (ELVC)**
    Field of Application: Relationship Economics **Summary:** Analyzes invisible work, empathy as unpaid labor, and the elasticity of patience. **KPI:** Number of thankless tasks before detonation.
15. **The Breakup Repositioning Model (BRM)**
    Field of Application: Brand Management **Summary:** A three-phase framework for post-relationship rebranding:
    1. Shock absorption,
    2. Narrative control,
    3. Personal re-launch. **Outcome:** Identity pivot, usually to wellness content.
16. **The Laundry Optimization Process (LOP)**
    Field of Application: Operational Efficiency **Summary:** Batch-processing methodology for repetitive domestic tasks. **Cycle:** Sort → Wash → Forget → Rewash.

17. **The Gossip Network Intelligence Model (GNIM)**
Field of Application: Informal Communication Systems **Summary:** Studies rumor propagation as a decentralized data-sharing protocol. **Finding:** Accuracy inversely proportional to entertainment value.
18. **The Strategic Inaction Quadrant (SIQ)**
Field of Application: Decision Science **Summary:** Plots opportunity cost against serenity. **Insight:** Doing nothing is often the most productive option — but only if done confidently.
19. **The Existential KPI Dashboard (EKD)**
Field of Application: Meaning Management **Summary:** An absurd yet oddly practical template for measuring fulfillment, clarity, and caffeine intake. **Outcome:** Red, always red.
20. **The Grand Strategy of Doing Life Poorly, But With Style (GSDLPWS)**
Field of Application: Meta-Philosophy **Summary:** A unifying framework for embracing imperfection as brand identity. **Strategic Objective:** Graceful failure. **Core Insight:** If you can't win, be interesting while losing.

Note: All models have been validated through extensive anecdotal research, primarily conducted in kitchens, queues, and emotional aftermaths. Replication is strongly encouraged and statistically meaningless.

GLOSSARY OF TERMS

(A Survival Dictionary for the Strategically Overwhelmed)

Compiled by the Institute for Applied Overthinking, in collaboration with several tired people pretending to understand economics.

Accountability Theatre

The performance of responsibility without the inconvenience of results. Common in group projects, meetings, and family WhatsApp groups.

Adaptive Burnout

The ability to remain functional while quietly disintegrating, often mistaken for "resilience." Usually accompanied by phrases like *"It's fine, I just need to get through this week."*

Algorithmic Guilt

That familiar shame triggered by recommendation engines reminding you what you "might also like," especially while procrastinating self-improvement.

Ambition Inflation

The steady rise of expectations with no corresponding increase in capability or energy. The invisible economic engine of LinkedIn.

Behavioral Arbitrage

The act of exploiting inconsistencies in one's own logic for temporary emotional profit. Example: "I deserve this cake because I skipped lunch," said while eating lunch.

Bounded Rationality

A polite term for "doing the best you can with the little time, patience, and caffeine you have left."

Cognitive Overdraft

Spending tomorrow's energy on today's decisions. Interest rates vary according to guilt and calendar notifications.

Decision Fatigue

The progressive erosion of judgment caused by choosing between equally disappointing options (e.g., food delivery apps or potential life partners).

Delegation Illusion

The belief that assigning a task to someone else has any long-term effect on your own stress levels.

Deliverable Drift

When a simple task acquires new objectives, sub-objectives, and philosophical weight until it collapses under its own ambition. Also known as *Tuesday.*

Emotional ROI (Return on Irritation)

The ratio of satisfaction gained to frustration invested in a relationship, project, or online debate. Rarely positive, yet endlessly recalculated.

Empathy Fatigue

A chronic condition caused by caring more than one's bandwidth allows. Often treated with sarcasm or selective disappearance.

Existential KPI

A non-measurable performance metric that nonetheless determines your sense of worth. Example: "Am I doing enough?" (Answer: no, but neither is anyone else.)

Framework Fatigue

The exhaustion that sets in when every aspect of life is explained using diagrams, arrows, or quadrants. Symptoms include cynicism, doodling, and wine.

Incremental Enlightenment

The slow, often accidental realization that you might have been wrong since 2009 — but in interesting ways.

Influence Without Authority

A corporate euphemism meaning "convince people who don't report to you to do things they don't want to." Also describes parenting, dating, and group travel planning.

Information Asymmetry

The strategic advantage of knowing slightly more than others — or pretending to. Essential in office politics and trivia nights.

Innovation Fatigue

The emotional numbness resulting from too many brainstorming sessions that end in Post-it Notes and nothing else.

Marginal Utility of Happiness

The law stating that the second cup of coffee is always less satisfying than the first, but still entirely necessary for survival.

Micro-Optimization Syndrome

The tendency to improve trivial details while ignoring foundational chaos. E.g., color-coding your to-do list instead of doing it.

Narrative Arbitrage

Reinterpreting a failure as a "learning experience" for reputational gain. The preferred coping mechanism of most professionals and all philosophers.

Opportunity Cost of Sanity

The hidden price of pursuing ambition without pause. Payable in weekends, sleep, and small talk.

Passive-Aggressive Synergy

When two parties cooperate outwardly but quietly hope the other fails first. The foundation of most partnerships, marriages, and cross-functional teams.

Path Dependence

The psychological inertia that keeps you doing something just because you've been doing it — like maintaining subscriptions, relationships, or gym memberships.

Performative Humility

The art of pretending not to care about something you desperately want credit for. A core leadership competency on social media.

Portfolio of Regrets

A diversified collection of past decisions, optimally balanced for both nostalgia and shame.

Risk Appetite Fatigue

When your willingness to take chances collapses under accumulated disappointments and warranty claims.

Satisficing

Choosing something that's "good enough" instead of perfect, usually 15 minutes before a deadline or dinner reservation.

Scarcity of Stillness

A modern economic phenomenon wherein attention, not time, becomes the rarest resource.

Signal-to-Noise Ratio (Emotional Edition)

The proportion of meaningful human interaction to group chat notifications. Healthy ratio: 1:300.

Strategic Inaction

The intentional choice to do nothing, disguised as deep contemplation. The only tactic that always works eventually.

Synergy Fatigue

The cumulative exhaustion caused by repeated attempts to "collaborate" with people who should really just email you.

Virtue Signaling (Sustainable Edition)

The act of broadcasting moral choices for social capital, often offset by the carbon footprint of your self-righteousness.

Win-Win Delusion

The comforting myth that compromise leaves everyone happy. In practice: two people equally disappointed, but professionally polite about it.

All definitions are subject to interpretation, context, and caffeine levels. No liability accepted for life choices made after reading this glossary.

READER'S GUIDE TO STRATEGIC LIVING

(Condensed Notes from a Lifetime of Overthinking)

"Life is not a zero-sum game — it's just that nobody told the people keeping score." — N. Mohanayak, during a particularly long family dinner.

I. Strategic Principles for Everyday Existence

1. **Assume Rational Irrationality.** Everyone, including you, is making the best possible decision under the worst possible assumptions. Strategy begins when you stop expecting consistency and start optimizing chaos.
2. **Seek Equilibrium, Not Harmony.** Harmony requires mutual understanding; equilibrium just needs both sides to be equally tired. Most domestic peace treaties rely on this insight.
3. **Every Decision Has an Aftertaste.** Like reheated pizza, some choices seem brilliant at 2 AM but questionable under sunlight. Factor in regret as a recurring cost, not a one-time charge.
4. **Strategy ≠ Control.** The universe runs on stochastic processes and mild irony. The best you can do is look purposeful while improvising.
5. **Plan Like a General, Act Like a Comedian.** There's no such thing as a perfect move — only well-timed self-awareness.

II. The Laws of Domestic Diplomacy

1. **Game Theory Is Real, Especially in the Kitchen.** The optimal outcome in household chores is mutual deflection balanced by selective amnesia.

2. **Porter's Five Forks Applies to Every Dinner Table.**
    - Bargaining power of the chef.
    - Threat of leftovers.
    - Rivalry among critics.
    - Substitutes: Takeout, cereal, resignation.
3. **Stakeholder Management Begins at Home.** If you can navigate in-laws, you can handle mergers. The only difference is that quarterly reviews are called "family gatherings."
4. **Beware the Weekend Project Fallacy.** Hope is not a building material.

III. The Commuter's Codex

1. **Every Traffic Jam Is a Systems Problem.** Too many inputs, too little throughput, and a complete lack of feedback loops — much like your department.
2. **Queue Theory Is a Moral Lesson.** The other line *will* move faster. It's not karma; it's just math with a sense of humor.
3. **The Umbrella Hedge Fund Model.** Always carry one. The ROI of smug dryness outperforms any market.
4. **Strategic Patience Is Not Laziness.** It's simply waiting for others to prove you were right all along.

IV. The Social Supply Chain

1. **Friendship Has a Portfolio Risk Profile.** Diversify emotional investments. Too much exposure to one person and your stability index collapses.
2. **Reciprocity Is Not a Linear Function.** Favors depreciate; gratitude accrues slowly. Manage your goodwill liquidity wisely.
3. **Signaling Is Inevitable.** Even silence is a message — usually, "I'm ignoring you strategically."

4. **The ROI on Kindness May Be Delayed.** But the compounding effect is remarkable — unless you keep spreadsheets on it, in which case it vanishes instantly.

V. The Market Inside Your Mind

1. **Impulse Control Is Behavioral Fiction.** Retail therapy works for 17 minutes; buyer's remorse lasts until the next payday.
2. **Subscriptions Are the New Serfdom.** Small debits make for large despair. Audit yourself before your bank does.
3. **Brand Loyalty Equals Emotional Captivity.** If you think your phone brand is a moral identity, blink twice for help.
4. **Minimalism Is Just Maximalist Signaling.** "Having less" is now a competitive sport — best observed, not joined.

VI. The Relationship Economy

1. **Love Is a Multi-Sided Market.** Matching algorithms can't fix asymmetric expectations.
2. **Negotiation Is Romance in Excel.** Track concessions. Audit silences. Budget apologies.
3. **Emotional Labor Has Hidden Costs.** Every "it's fine" is a deferred payment. Interest compounds.
4. **Breakups Are Strategic Divestments.** Exit with dignity, rebrand with humor, pivot to introspection.

VII. The Corporate Mirror

1. **Laundry = Operations.** Batch, delay, repeat. Efficiency emerges through shame.
2. **Parenting = Talent Development.** Feedback loops, performance reviews, occasional resignations.
3. **Gossip = Informal Knowledge Network.** Faster than Slack, more accurate than official communication.
4. **Doing Nothing = Strategic Slack.** Inaction is the soul's R&D department.

VIII. Meta-Strategy: How to Think Strategically About Thinking Strategically

1. **Frameworks Are Decorative.** They make confusion look professional.
2. **Every Plan Devolves into Improvisation.** The key is to appear as if you meant it.
3. **Self-Help Is the Final Boss.** The only strategy book that makes money is the one telling others how to strategize.
4. **Remember: "Doing Life Poorly, But With Style" Is Still a Strategy.** Competence is overrated; coherence is optional; comic timing is eternal.

IX. Post-Scriptum for the Over-Earnest

If at any point in this book you found a profound truth, it's likely an accident. If you laughed instead, congratulations — you understood it perfectly.

THE FINAL FRAMEWORK

Here's the only diagram you'll ever need:

Figure ∞. The Life Strategy Loop

1. Observe.
2. Overthink.
3. Laugh.
4. Adjust nothing.
5. Repeat until enlightenment or lunch, whichever comes first.

Thank you for reading. Now go live badly — but strategically.

(Signed, with mild regret and unshakable affection, Navoch Mohanayak.)